BAR
Excellence

DESIGNS FOR PUBS & CLUBS

BAR
Excellence

DESIGNS FOR PUBS & CLUBS

Christy Casamassima

PBC International Inc

Distributor to the book trade in the
United States and Canada
Rizzoli International Publications Inc.
through St. Martin's Press
175 Fifth Avenue
New York, NY 10010

Distributor to the book trade outside the
United States and Canada
Hearst Books International
1350 Avenue of the Americas
New York, NY 10019

All other distribution
PBC International Inc.
One School Street
Glen Cove, NY 11542

Write or phone for our free catalog
PBC International Inc.
One School Street
Glen Cove, NY 11542
1-800-527-2826
within NY State 516-676-2727

Library of Congress Cataloging-in-Publication Data
Casamassima, Christy.
    Bar excellence : designs for pubs & clubs /
    by Christy Casamassima.
        p.   cm.
    Includes index.
    ISBN 0-86636-680-6 (hardcover)
    1. Bars (Drinking establishments)—Decoration.
    2. Interior decoration—History—20th century.
    3. Interior architecture—History—20th century.
    I. Title.
    NK2195.R4   1999
    725.72—dc21   CIP
                                                   99-2843

CAVEAT—Information in this text is believed accu-
rate, and will pose no problem for the student or
casual reader. However, the author was often
constrained by information contained in signed
release forms, information that could have been
in error or not included at all. Any misinformation
(or lack of information) is the result of failure in these
attestations. The author has done whatever is
possible to insure accuracy.

10 9 8 7 6 5 4 3 2 1

Printed in Hong Kong.

To my husband,
Douglas Robert Colasurdo, with love,

Christy

contents

foreword

Glamour and comfort are back, and I, for one, am glad to see it. This is what the nightclub experience should be about. In conceiving several of the projects in this book, I wanted to create places that would put the style back into going out. To invite people to dress up, meet old friends and make new

ones in an environment that inspires, intrigues, and gives a comfortable ambience to the social nature that inhabits us all.

It is said that everything that is old becomes new again. That which is held dear by a generation will fall out of favor with the next, only to be rediscovered and reinvented by those that follow. We see the ebb and flow of the collective taste expressed in design, architecture, fashion, and politics.

As the century draws to a close, we have come full circle in the expression of style and taste. From the lush nightclubs of the '30s and '40s to the streamlined modern of the '50s, to the cathartic high art of the '60s, the bombast of the '70s, to the self-service of the '80s, and back again to the lush comfort of the '90s.

Yet in the bar of the '90s we can see all aspects of the cycle. While for some it is

a refuge to relax and unwind from the stress of the working day, for others it is a place for adventure and the excitement of new acquaintances. It is a meeting place for adults where a man (or a woman) can smoke a great cigar, have a cocktail (martini preferred), and inhabit for a few hours the good life that is sought by the heart of all of us.

The experience should be one of empowerment to the patron no matter who he or she is. All aspects of the design should contribute to this—colors, fabrics, and, perhaps most importantly, the lighting should combine along with the service to make a person look and feel their absolute best.

An executive entertaining clients, the couple drinking champagne, or friends arguing the issues of the day—for a few hours they are all celebrities.

Margaret O'Brien
O'Brien + Associates Design Inc.

introduction

Time was, the neighborhood tavern functioned as an intimate social hub, a gritty gathering place for friends and coworkers to let off steam, celebrate, meet and mingle, or keep up with local gossip. That was back in the day when a bar was a bar, from which patrons expected nothing more than a cold beer, a friendly face, and an empty stool. Not anymore. Today's

overworked urbanites harbor heightened expectations when it comes to a night on the town. With their incredibly shrinking leisure time, consumers place great store in their decision of where to meet for a drink. Invariably, they demand more for their discretionary dollar. In the end, the dark, smoky pub simply can't hold a candle to the competition.

The longing for the stylish noir atmosphere reminiscent of the '40s has spawned a retro revival. To keep up with the trend, restaurateurs and bar owners are their venues in order to make space for swank martini bars and cozy cigar lounges. These luxe spaces are a toast to the highlife. Decked in plush velvets and rich woods, today's see-and-be-seen retro lounges make patrons feel that they've "arrived." Stiff drinks—and stiffer tariffs—create a clubby air of exclusivity and privilege.

Of course, the new breed of bars has nothing on the grande dames, which are discreetly tucked away in exclusive hotels. These old-world enclaves have been pouring premium libations to

the sophisticated traveler in distinguished surroundings for ages. Hotel bars are still among your best bets for the consummate cocktail without fancy names, gimmicks, or marketing ploys.

For beer drinkers, a proliferation of contemporary microbreweries offers a laundry list of boutique beers on draft, as well as bright, congenial settings, often featuring gargantuan copper brewing vats at center stage.

Then there's the multifarious nightspot—a hybrid that combines elements to create a destination where drinking, dancing, lounging, dining, and socializing converge under one roof. In general, the nightspot pays homage to the technical advances of our era, employing state-of-the-art sound and light systems to their full potential.

And, of course, the '90s is the era of the theme bar, drawing much inspiration from the worlds of sports, music, fashion, and movies—to name a few. These ubiquitous bar/restaurants attract a youthful crowd seeking entertainment and a glimpse into celebrity and pop culture.

Christy Casamassima

Living Room
São Paulo, Brazil

LIKE MANY POPULAR NIGHTSPOTS, LIVING ROOM CAPITALIZES ON THE DEMAND FOR A SOPHISTICATED, UPSCALE ENVIRONMENT FOR A MATURE AUDIENCE INTERESTED IN FINE WINE, GOOD MUSIC, AND PREMIUM CIGARS. A HOPPING SÃO PAULO ENCLAVE, LIVING ROOM CATERS TO A SMART AND SAVVY CLIENTELE WITH A YEN FOR COCKTAILS AND SOCIALIZING IN A TASTEFULLY SUBDUED ATMOSPHERE. THE

architect's penchant for soft colors and natural light is reflected in the contemporary and spare surroundings. High ceilings lend a sense of expanse to the otherwise cozy setup, and the use of tiny inset spotlights make the natural brick walls the center of attention. Along one wall, a clever built-in wine cellar is set over the main bar. The backlit liquor shelving allows the bar area to beckon with an alluring glow. Modern seating alcoves are generally filled with small groups of

revelers enjoying a fine cigar or an after dinner cocktail. Rectangular tube lighting between booths cleverly separates seating areas and provides illumination on each of the tables. From floor to ceiling, a language of rich materials—genuine wool, marble, and wood—all speak for themselves. Club patrons are immersed in a sanctuary filled with tempered light, customized furnishings, and a smattering of elegant details, in a space that doesn't rely on gimmicks nor shock value.

architect/interior designer: Studio Arthur de Mattos Casas
square feet/meters: 3,337/310 • design budget: $310,000 • seats: 80
photographer: Tuca Reinés

The striking features of the bar/lounge area are a utilitarian wine bar suspended overhead, built-in booths surrounded by custom chairs, and natural elements, such as exposed brick walls and wood detailing • Instead of relying on flashy art, antiques, plants, or other decorative accessories, the designer chose to let the room's natural materials and custom lighting make a grand gesture of understated yet contemporary style.

The Summit
Tulsa, Oklahoma

THE DESIGN CONCEPT FOR THE SUMMIT WAS TO CREATE A WELCOMING AND FRIENDLY GROUP OF SPACES THAT FLOW TOGETHER, EACH TAKING ADVANTAGE OF THE VIEWS OF TULSA FROM THE PENTHOUSE FLOOR OF THE NATIONSBANK BUILDING. THE CLIENTS DESIRED A WARM AND COMFORTABLE VENUE, BUT ALSO REQUIRED A SPACE THAT COULD LIVE UP TO THIS PRIVATE CLUB'S UPSCALE

reputation. The major challenge for Taylor Scott Architects and Synar Design Group was to create distinct spaces that exploit fantastic panoramic views without being merely "rooms with a view." An aura of intimacy was achieved with sensual spaces for cocktails, dining, entertaining, cigar smoking, and lounging. A special request made by club members was that the existing teak flooring and wall panels, and the coffered teak ceiling in the bar be preserved. In fact, the teak was reused after being removed and refinished. The "historic" wood was reinstalled without the brass

details. Although the quantity of paneling was reduced, the detailed grain was preserved. There was great concern that major renovation would destroy a space that had seen a great many transactions in the oil industry. As a result, the fireplace, the Andean black granite bar top and other original details of significance were retained. To enhance the flow between spaces, curvilinear archways and an open layout were used. An Italian courtyard-style lobby, cigar lounge, built-in wine cellar, and an array of lushly upholstered furnishings add panache.

architect: **Taylor Scott Architects** • interior Designer: **Synar Design Group**
square feet/meters: **8,536/793** • design budget: not disclosed • seats: **194** • check average: **$75**
photographer: **Reyndell Stockman**

The commodious and inviting lounge area offers a spacious retreat. Intimate details, such as the original fireplace, a built-in wine display, and soft candles, create the warm and personal ambience that makes club members feel at home. • Teak accents and an arched entry are visual ties that link the bar with the other club spaces. Curved moldings lead the eye around the ceiling.

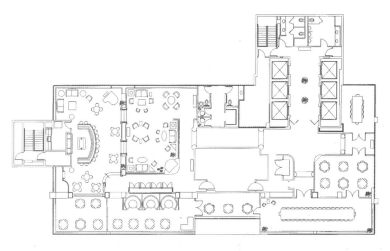

Michael's Club
Celebrity Cruises Galaxy Liner

THE PARTNERS OF CELEBRITY CRUISES, RECOGNIZING THE CACHET OF CIGAR BARS, INSTALLED AN URBANE AND UPSCALE VERSION IN THEIR GALAXY LINER. INSTEAD OF RE-CREATING THE DARK, MASCULINE ATMOSPHERE OF A MEN'S CLUB, THE ARCHITECTS CHOSE TO CREATE A DISTINGUISHED GATHERING SPOT FOR MEMBERS OF BOTH SEXES. A PLACE TO ENJOY A FINE STOGIE IN PRIVATE, THE

enclosed space is distinguished from the rest of the ship while respecting its original style. The architects' main challenge was to establish an intimate space in a curious, 1,200-square-foot diagonal room adjacent to a five-story atrium. The first step was to erect a curved row of blond wood columns and a leather-clad entry to signal the transition from the adjoining atrium. A definitive circular room is anchored by a curving row of bookcases and framed by custom curving banquettes finished in a rich red velvet. Nearby, the back wall is a free-floating glass curtain which is lit from behind, separating the outside and instilling a sense of

timelessness within. The whimsical white perforated ceiling panels are recessed to create an illusion of added height and a visual connection to the omnipresent porthole windows. Along the perimeter of the main space, seating is broken into clusters of plush navy chairs around white cocktail tables. Centrally located white sofas offer an inviting spot to savor cocktails in a more informal setting. The walls, of fine anigré wood, oppose the use of heavy mahogany that one tends to associate with masculine smoking lounges of yesteryear. Nautical colors and clean, contemporary elements give the space a fresh appeal.

architect/interior designer: **Shelton, Mindel & Associates**
square feet/meters: **1,200/111** • design budget: not disclosed • seats: **45**
photographer: **Dan Cornish**

In the confines of an awkward space, the architects managed to use the curving angles to their advantage. The recessed ceiling cutouts provide added height to increase the perception of space. • The spartan elegance is enhanced by couches, navy seating groupings, and traditional wall sconces. The translucent windows focus patrons' attention inside the room as opposed to the rest of the ship which prompts the eye toward the water.

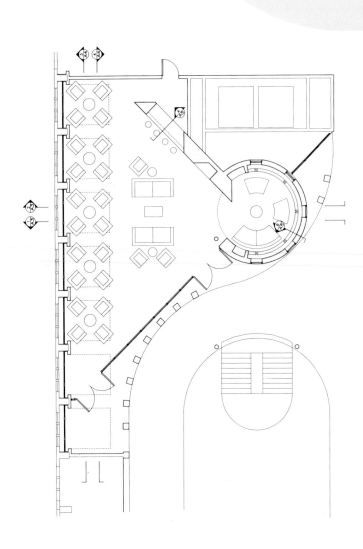

Fusion
Toronto, Ontario

AN INTRIGUING, HIP DESIGN IS CREDITED FOR THE SUCCESS OF FUSION—AN ENERGIZED, MODERN CLUB THAT TRANSCENDS THE ORIGINAL STRUCTURE'S INHERENT LIMITATIONS. ALTHOUGH THE UNDERGROUND SITE WAS POORLY CONFIGURED, THE DESIGNERS CLEVERLY INTEGRATED FUTURISTIC AND MODERN ELEMENTS FOR AN ATMOSPHERE WELL DESERVING OF ITS ECLECTIC NAME. BELOW GRADE, THE SITE HAD

low ceilings and was awkwardly constructed. The design challenge was to make this space work with minimal renovation and a small budget. The owners wanted to maintain a sense of vastness while defining separate areas for mingling, lounging, and dancing. A compact lobby introduces "the tunnel"—a large entrance space leading to a series of lounges which culminates with the dance floor. Only a few narrow partitions define the spaces. Iridescent vinyl curtains flank the perimeter walls, custom area rugs decorate the floors, and retro chairs give a hip edge. On the outside of the partition separating the circular VIP

lounge from the main bar area, bubble mirrors (typically used for security purposes) distort views and refract images, creating an ever-changing wall of art. Mirrored slats on the lounge walls provide optical distortion and a "fun house" atmosphere. The upholstered lounge benches are interrupted by inset tempered glass drink surfaces that are illuminated from below. Another unique feature includes freestanding dividers composed of holographic vinyl that are lit from both top and bottom. These are individually controlled by concealed motors, which produce hypnotic, wave-like motions. Fiberoptic flowers also change colors to the music.

interior designer: II BY IV Design Associates Inc.
square feet/meters: 8,200/762 • design budget: $328,000
photographer: David Whittaker

The large lounge area is a study in simplicity. Upholstered benches are accompanied by flush drink tables, which are cleverly lit from underneath to provide a spaceship glow. The perimeter of iridescent vinyl drapery is a low-budget technique used to cover the walls and add a dash of flash. ● The futuristic entrance tunnel leads to a massive gathering space. Curved holographic panels shimmer with color and reflect an iridescent, mystical aura. ● Funky stools and retro chairs are scattered throughout. The simple concrete floor is made interesting through the addition of color and the reflection of light.

V2

London, England

THE CONCEPT FOR V2, A PRIVATE CLUB WITHIN THE CORPORATE HEADQUARTERS OF RICHARD BRANSON'S NEW RECORD COMPANY, REFLECTS HIS PHILOSOPHY OF MIXING BUSINESS AND PLEASURE. BRANSON SOUGHT A HIP PROFESSIONAL CENTER THAT COULD DOUBLE AS AN ENTERTAINMENT FACILITY FOR CLIENTS, STAFF, AND GUESTS IN THE RECORD INDUSTRY. AS SUCH, THE DESIGN NEEDED TO BLEND ELEMENTS

from the corporate world, such as a professional reception area, with elements of a youthful, private club. The designers balanced the dual nature of the space—a historic building with an old London sensibility, which was equipped for the latest technology. Upon entry, the reception area doubles as a stand-up bar, making a social gathering a possibility at a moment's notice. The desk is adorned with antique movable wood type, cleverly reflected by the corporate logo which beckons from a fish tank behind the bar. Downstairs, the space comfortably integrates funky

industry gatherings in a private club atmosphere. Since the lounge originally had low ceilings and a lack of natural light, the area was visually expanded with space-enhancing colors. The ceiling mural, duplicated from a turn-of-the-century Russian Constructivist film poster, also broadens the perspective. Lending a touch of whimsy are words from *Alice in Wonderland*. All of the areas are wired for closed-circuit television and hi-tech sound—one of Branson's key requests. The design, furnishings, and mood truly reflect his groundbreaking vision and personality.

interior designer: Ergo Design Works Inc.
square feet/meters: 5,000/465 • design budget: not disclosed • seats: 40
photographer: Richard Bryant

By day, the reception desk, inlaid with woodblock lettering, is used for traditional purposes, but it easily doubles as a bar for spontaneous parties and entertaining. Silkscreen window treatments were designed by a London artist. • The downstairs lounge/entertainment area, with bar, piano, and suspended televisions, makes a simple yet sophisticated statement. Floors are inlaid with a colorful geometric pattern which corresponds with the purple hues on doors, blinds, and other interior detailing.

Magazzini Generali
Milan, Italy

THE OWNERS OF MAGAZZINI GENERALI WANTED TO CREATE A HIP, HARMONIOUS AND FLOWING SPACE, WHERE PEOPLE OF ALL AGES AND BACKGROUNDS COULD FEEL WELCOME. THE IDEA WAS TO BUILD A PLACE THAT IS INFORMAL, SPARE, AND RESPECTS THE INDUSTRIAL ARCHAEOLOGY OF THE TURN OF THE CENTURY. THE WAREHOUSE SPACE WAS IDEAL FOR MULTIFARIOUS PURPOSES INCLUDING

exhibitions, live performances, and pure socializing. In keeping with the original industrial character, designers chose to use pared-down materials with warm and base colors. The two-story space is connected by an internal staircase. The main floor houses a bar, stage, and two production booths. The gently curved main floor bar is a simple affair, rendered in steel and wood. Large globe lanterns playfully suspended from the ceiling direct the eye around the bar as it sweeps into the main floor lounge areas. To decrease the daunting scale of the warehouse-style room, the

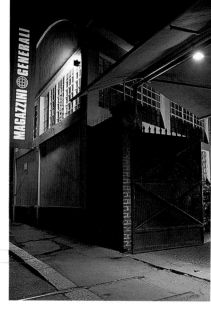

designers used large colorful soffits, painted exposed piping, and suspended TVs as points of interest. A raised lounge area is cordoned off by metal railings, which set apart groupings of custom designed chairs. The underground bar is a bit more colorful, accented with red, deep and pale blue walls. Mini spotlights provide soft, diffused lighting, perfect for showcasing dancers. Due to the range of performances staged here, the sound and lighting systems play an integral role in enhancing the artists and the surrounding areas.

architects: Gian Carlo Soresina, S-R-1, s.r.l. • Massimo Josa Ghini
interior designers: Gian Carlo Soresina, S-R-1, s.r.l. • Davide Mercatali
square feet/meters: 18,000/1,674 • design budget: $1 million • seats: 200
photographer: © Magazzini Generali Milano. Photo by Beck Peccoz/Fasano

The main floor bar area initiates a series of gentle curves that undulates through the space. Poured concrete flooring and exposed rafters were employed to enhance the industrial effect. • The dance floor is housed underground, and illuminated by simple spot lighting. • From another angle, the main bar is a study in simplicity. A DJ booth is suspended above, as are simple paper globe lights. • The bar on the lower level is injected with splashes of color.

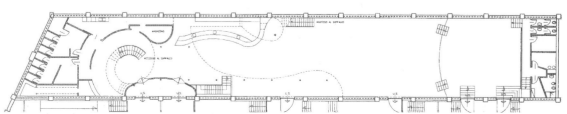

The Gate
Los Angeles, California

AFTER THE GATE, A WILDLY POPULAR DINNER AND DANCE CLUB, BURNED DOWN IN 1996, THE DESIGNER ACCEPTED THE CHALLENGE OF CREATING AN EVEN MORE EXQUISITE SPACE FOR DINING, DANCING, AND LOUNGING. TODAY, PATRONS STEP THROUGH THE IMPOSING ARCHED, WROUGHT-IRON ENTRANCE INTO AN OTHER WORLD OF BYZANTINE, RENAISSANCE, AND FRENCH MODERN STYLES.

The site has become a favorite among the entertainment industry for celebrations and location shoots. From the outside, patrons are transfixed by this remarkable structure, watched over by gargoyle sentries affixed to stone pillars. Bird's-eye maple, trompe l'oeil artwork, colonnades, velveteen draped partitions, and Renaissance chandeliers greet visitors with incomparable elegance. A Baroque chandelier illuminates the entry from an inset dome which is glazed in gold leaf. Further inside, the original art, antiques, and intimate seating areas evoke images of a European mansion.

Flanking either side of a stone fireplace, French doors lead to a secluded patio enclosed by wrought-iron grillwork. Patrons travel through rooms of various sizes, all of which lead to a disco surrounded by three complete bars. Perched slightly above the dance floor is a lush lounge, or Gallery Room, which has its own entrance, bar, estate hearth, and slated patio. Velvet curtains separate rooms, private alcoves, and elaborately stocked libraries. The acoustics and disco lighting are state-of-the-art, and the exhaust system was enhanced to eliminate cigar smoke and circulate air.

architect/interior designer: O'Brien + Associates Design Inc.
square feet/meters: 8,000/743 • design budget: $1 million • seats: 300 • check average: $50
photographer: Paul Dennler

Curved wrought-iron grillwork subtly separates the dance floor from the adjoining lounge and bar areas. • The diverse layout is designed to unfold as the evening develops. Although the bars, lounges, and discos are separated into sections by visual cues and textural changes, all are open to encourage the see-and-be-seen interaction. • Cozy club chairs are arranged in small seating clusters to afford private spaces for intimate conversations. The luxe decor and inviting details of this library suggest a private mansion.

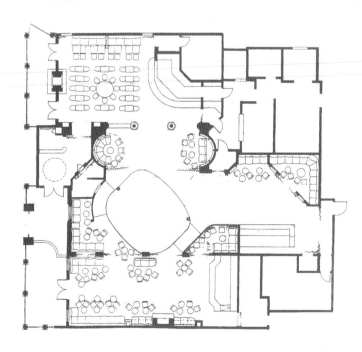

Luxor Palace
Dresden, Germany

APTLY NAMED, LUXOR PALACE EXHIBITS THE GRANDEUR AND IMPOSING DIMENSIONS OF AN EXOTIC EGYPTIAN TEMPLE. THE GOAL WAS TO ATTRACT A YOUNG, INTELLECTUAL CLIENTELE UNACQUAINTED WITH TRAVELING. HENCE, LUXOR PALACE IS INTENDED TO TRANSPORT PATRONS TO AN ANCIENT, MYSTICAL WORLD, IF ONLY FOR THE EVENING. ONE OF THE MOST PERVASIVE DESIGN ELEMENTS EMPLOYED

throughout the space is one of symmetry, order and balance. A starry night motif on the carpeting is echoed on the ceiling while opposing walls continue this theme with centered sconces. Pin lights in the dark-hued ceiling creates the effect of stars twinkling in the night sky. In the dining area, low-voltage directional spotlights were used to avoid a harsh glare. One of the greatest disadvantages of this

project was that Dresden did not offer a pool of craftsmen from which to draw. French artisans were called upon for their expertise and for many of the materials. The plaster, carpeting, furniture—even the terrazzo paint had to be imported. The exotic Egyptian motif is magnificently executed through iron grillwork, stone sculptures, hand-painted murals, and the ubiquitous image of the lotus flower.

architect/interior designer: Jean-Pierre Heim & Associates Inc.
square feet/meters: 12,000/1,115 • design budget: $1.5 million • seats: 400
photographer: Fabrice Rambert

The multilevel facility is woven together with a keen eye towards symmetry and a consistent color palette. • A raised seating nook is arranged for intimate conversation. Overhead, the ornamented molding cleverly houses more point lighting. • Cafe tables atop a marble floor provide a place for respite at the bottom of a central stairway. Two reclining sphinxes appear to stand guard over the room.

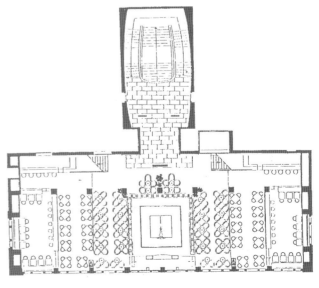

Cheeky Monkey Cafe
Newport, Rhode Island

DESIGNED WITH A BRITISH COLONIAL AURA ON THE WHARF IN NEWPORT, CHEEKY MONKEY CAFE IS A PROTOTYPE FOR OTHER UNITS ACROSS THE COUNTRY. THE THEME IS PLAYFUL AND HIGHLY VISUAL, FEATURING A FAMILY OF CUSTOM TROMPE L'OEIL OIL PORTRAITS OF MISCHIEVOUS MONKEYS, EACH WITH ITS OWN STORY. THE FANCIFUL MONKEYS AT PLAY SET THE STAGE FOR AN EXUBERANT VENUE THAT

serves equal parts food, fun, and entertainment. Originally a retail space with a "shopping mall" layout, the configuration of the site presented the greatest challenge since it is divided into three separate units: bar, dining room, and second-floor cigar lounge. The designers set out to present these distinct spaces in a unified manner, to provide for people-watching from all areas, and to create a setting that is amenable to fine dining. The kitchen sightline was elevated to allow patrons a view of the chef in action, while a mirrored banquette wall with animal print seats provides a visual divider. Two

large chef's food tables are also housed on the platform level to maximize the relationship between chef and customer. Particular attention was paid to the lighting of the restaurant with twelve-volt cables, sconces, and floor lamps which were customized to imbue the space with points of light and a warm glow. All finishes are faux painted to create a casual yet sophisticated feel. The visual intrigue of the space is enhanced by the extensive use of antiques, custom artwork, lighting, and accessories, all featuring the eccentricities of monkeys who enjoy high-society life.

interior designer: Maggie Gordon Design, Inc.
square feet/meters: 2,000/186 • design budget: $80,000 • seats: 126 • check average: $40
photographer: Ron Manville

The main bar and restaurant area are designed in the British tradition with simple wooden details. • The second-story lounge area was created as a relaxed hideaway for after dinner drinks. The animal print upholstery, clubby leather sofas, and oversized gilded mirrors provide chic comfort. • Lively oil portraits by artist Betsy Florin create a sense of novelty and spark conversation.

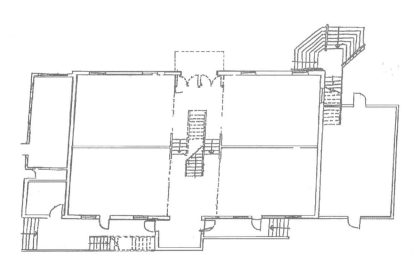

Zoom Caffe and Bar

Toronto, Ontario

IN A CITY ALREADY INUNDATED WITH FINE DINING ROOMS, A SUCCESSFUL CATERING FIRM ASKED II BY IV DESIGN ASSOCIATES TO HELP THEM CREATE A SOPHISTICATED ENVIRONMENT FOR WORLD-CLASS DINING. THE DESIGNERS TOOK INSPIRATION FROM THE EXISTING STRUCTURE, A FORMER BANK, AND USED THE BUILDING'S EXCEEDINGLY HIGH CEILINGS TO THEIR ADVANTAGE. RATHER THAN DISGUISE THE NATURE OF THE

site, designers strategically employed the volume of the space as a dramatic feature. Past a pair of imposing stainless steel doors, the tiny, low-height entryway permits a full view into the restaurant rising dramatically beyond. The main space is cleverly manipulated with different materials and furniture layouts to establish a more intimate aura. Custom globe lights suspended from the perforated ceiling add interest and visually decrease the ceiling height. The huge mirror hung at an angle against the kitchen wall affords diners a variety of perspectives on the busy room. More mirrors are fronted with fanciful

sculptures of aircraft cable, steel tubing, and "test tube" vases, topped with magnifying lenses which zoom in on the reflection behind. The clever use of lenses extends into the screened opening to the kitchen, the entrance railing, and the elaborate back bar. A low, curving partition delineates the dining and lounge areas. Lushly upholstered lounge seating, small cocktail tables, and the use of diverse floor finishes, (including stone inlaid with steel logos and small area rugs), create intimate, private spaces. Dramatic indigo drapery, color accents, and low muted lamps punctuate the softly elegant ambience.

interior designer: II BY IV Design Associates Inc.
square feet/meters: 4,200/390 • design budget: not disclosed • seats: 80
photographer: David Whittaker

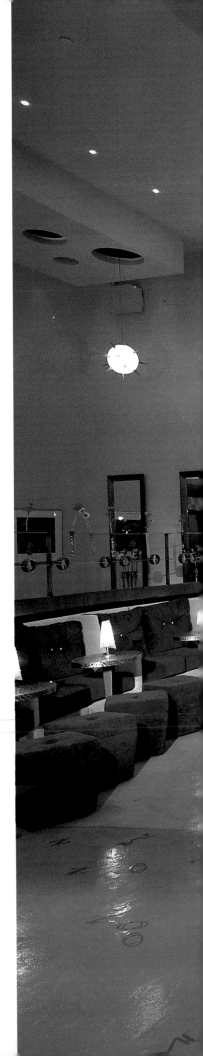

Although the space features dramatic ceiling heights, the designers achieved a sense of intimacy and human scale in a variety of ways. The lounge area is a series of small and cozy groupings of upholstered seating and low lamps. • The principal colors are vanilla, indigo, and gold set against natural stone and tinted concrete. Walnut was chosen for its visual weight and subtle, elegant grain, and the silver leaf wall finish and metal finishes throughout complement the underlying tone. • Suspended from cutouts in the ceiling, custom globe lighting with colorful spikes add a touch of whimsy. A chic and spartan bar enhances the rear wall with subtle lighting from behind.

g

New York, New York

Perhaps the lowercase "g" stands for gay in this upscale lounge for a mixed gay crowd. While gay bars of yesteryear were often hidden from the street, g provides an inviting new alternative. The bar is extremely sleek and clean, yet it exudes warmth through the full-height birch paneling and soft lighting. The space is divided into three distinct sections that flow into one another. With glass windows which open onto the street and an arched area for lounging, people-watching is anything but hidden. The transparent doors are etched with the lounge's logo, and the interior lighting delivers a warm glow and a view into the convivial assemblage. The architects' objective was to make the most of the existing arch to create the attractive focal point—a handsome elliptical bar at the center of the room. This gathering area serves for a lingering conversation or a quick stop before taking a seat on the spartan leather settees and ottomans in the intimate

interior lounge. The curved bar contrasts with the rectilinear forms of the lounge where stainless steel tables, stools, and bar fixtures are combined with warm and inviting leather furnishings. Since the architects wanted to create a lounge that was more sophisticated than most other places in the area, a strikingly simple mix of materials was implemented. Concrete, birch plywood, stainless steel, and ceramic tile make up the bold and modern palette. The use of theatrical lighting allows the owners to set the mood according to whim, and acoustical improvements keep the noise level down.

architect: James L. Bartholomew, Architect
square feet/meters: 3,500/325 • design budget: $525,000 • seats: 108
photographer: Wade Zimmerman

The sexy curved shape of the bar and the rounded soffit contrast nicely with the rectilinear forms of the adjoining lounge. • Soft paneled birch walls, left bare, are a light backdrop to the rich leather upholstered ottomans. Industrial details—poured concrete floors, birch walls, stainless bar stools and tables—evoke a sleek, contemporary sensibility.

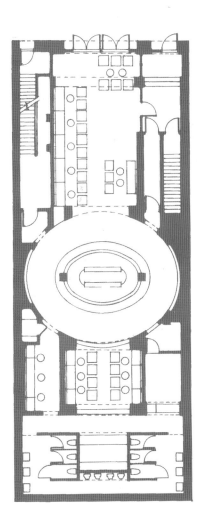

Michael Jordan's
Chicago, Illinois

CREATED TO "WOW" SPORTS FANS, THIS 18,000-SQUARE-FOOT VENUE IS MORE THAN JUST A RESTAURANT AND SPORTS BAR. IN FACT, THIS THREE-LEVEL ENTERTAINMENT EMPORIUM CONSISTS OF BAR, DINING ROOM, RETAIL SHOP, AND BANQUET FACILITY. FORGET ALL YOUR PREVIOUS ASSOCIATIONS WITH SPORTS BARS. THIS ELABORATE SHOWPLACE IS SLEEK, SOPHISTICATED, AND CONTEMPORARY.

The entrance provides clues to the scale of this project. A giant 18-foot basketball sits atop the building above a 30-by-30-foot banner of Air Jordan in motion. The bar, located on the first floor, is the main draw, with a $350,000 video wall that offers state-of-the-art sports coverage (not just the Bulls). Panoramic color photos of the crowd-filled Chicago stadium hang on either side of the wall. A three-tier skybox bar area offers prime viewing, while the main bar serving appetizers and sandwiches accommodates up to 150 people.

Black ceramic floor tile complements a 35-foot dark wood bar lit by cobalt neon lights. The walls display a range of artwork and memorabilia related to Jordan's career and sports achievements; *Sports Illustrated* covers featuring Jordan; an array of team jerseys from countries around the world— Italy, Japan, Hungary, Yugoslavia, Angola; and Jordan's trophies, awards, and championship rings. Portrait lamps illuminate the showpieces, each displayed with a sepia-toned event photo and a description of the prize, to help the viewer identify it.

interior designer: Zakaspace
square feet/meters: 17,775/1,651 • design budget: $3.9 million • seats: 475
photographer: Mark Ballogg © Steinkamp/Ballogg Chicago

Built to simulate stadium skyboxes, these elevated areas provide an excellent view of the oversized video screens at the bar. • A view into the handsome dining area, which displays fan mail from around the world and an array of magazine covers featuring Jordan over the years. The restaurant features an art collection which includes eight works by muralist Greg Gove. • The sweeping main bar is lit by track lighting. The extensive video system over the sleek wooden counter is the room's main attraction.

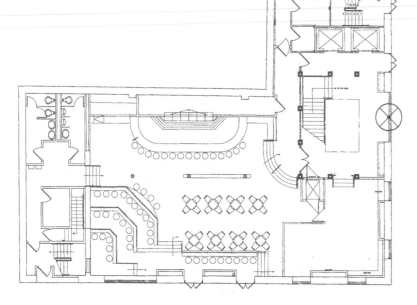

Speakeasy
Austin, Texas

RECALLING THE SPEAKEASIES OF THE '30S IN DOWNTOWN CHICAGO AND NEW YORK CITY, THE OWNERS SET OUT TO RE-CREATE THE MOOD OF A BYGONE ERA WITH A DIMLY LIT, SOMEWHAT MYSTERIOUS AND JAZZY ATMOSPHERE. WITH THESE OBJECTIVES IN MIND, THE ARCHITECTS AND DESIGNERS BEGAN THEIR RESEARCH. THE RESULT IS THIS UPDATED CLASSIC IN THE HEART OF AUSTIN. MANY OF THE DETAILS

of the original structure were employed to evoke the gritty, backdoor ambience of the clandestine speakeasies of the '30s. Poured concrete flooring, exposed brick walls, and un-painted rafters are juxtaposed with deep velvet curtains and lux-urious materials. The slightly decadent and mysterious mood is expressed throughout with details and fin-ishes, as in the highly polished wood bar, paneling, and trim. The dark hued color palette of deep bur-

gundy is offset by hanging fixtures, sconces, and ceiling fans. Lighting was

custom designed to reflect a period sensibility and evoke a sense of refuge. The mezzanine and entertainment area, however, are a nod to the present, featuring a simple acoustical ceil-ing which helps to minimize sound trans-mission. The space provides an ideal show-case for jazz musicians and a variety of per-formers. One of the owner's key requests was that Speakeasy feature a roof deck for outdoor enjoyment; a dream fullfilled when the roof was torn off and replaced with deck floor trusses.

architect: **Dick Clark Architecture** • interior designer: **Creative Consultants**
square feet/meters: 7,285/677 • design budget: not disclosed • seats: 400 • check average: $50
photographer: **Paul Bardagjy**

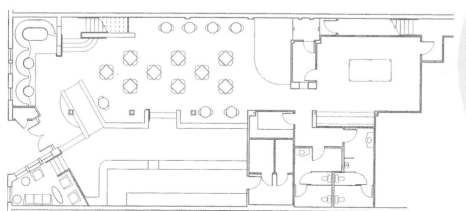

The entertainment area provides a showcase for jazz musicians and a variety of performers. The space is defined by exposed rafters, brick walls, and poured concrete floors. • The oversized windows frame the curved black leather banquettes. • The polished wood bar is offset by an exposed brick wall, repeating a theme of luxurious materials paired with gritty industrial elements. • The mezzanine level, surrounded by a custom railing, provides a view into the bar and cocktail area below.

Props
Charlotte, North Carolina

DESIGNED SPECIFICALLY TO MATCH THE ECLECTIC AND EXUBERANT TASTES OF GENERATION X, PROPS IS PURE FANTASY. ALTHOUGH THE BAR AREA APPEARS RATHER SUBDUED, THE RESTAURANT TAKEN AS A WHOLE IS A THEATRICAL MASTER-PIECE. THE CONCEPT IS BASED ON THE RADICALLY NEW EATING, DRINKING, AND SOCIALIZING HABITS OF THE YOUTH CULTURE. WITH A THEME IN MIND OF CREATING

a series of living room vignettes to promote social interaction, the first challenge for the designers was to completely renovate the existing restaurant, which had limited visibility and no parking. A highly visible awning system with silhouette letters was designed to create street presence in compliance with signage ordinance limitations, while a massive jack-in-the-box hanging from

the exposed rafters above the hostess stand conveys an idea of the fun that awaits patrons further inside. The expansive 13,000-square-foot area gave designers an extremely large

canvas on which to work. Polished wood floors are left bare, and colorfully painted walls are separated by heavy velvet curtains. The use of theatrical effects, such as stage lighting, curtains, and elevated stage platforms also contributes to the sense of theater. The bar and dining areas are the only two places in which more subdued elements, such as white tablecloths, and simplistic design come into play. Otherwise, one can expect to be surprised by a panoply of unusual flea market finds, from leopard-print chairs to retro lamps.

architect/interior designer: Shook Design Group, Inc.
square feet/meters: 13,000/1,207 • design budget: not disclosed • seats: 300 • check average: $21
photographer: Tim Buchman

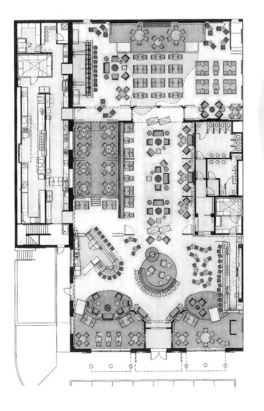

"Eat, Drink, Relax" exclaims the signage on the bold yellow awnings, while large windows offer a welcoming view of the interior. • The entrance into the dining room reveals how designers integrated the industrial qualities of the existing structure, such as the "loading dock" entryway to the more stylish, white tablecloth dining room. • Comfortable living room vignettes enhance the convivial atmosphere. • A gargantuan technicolor jack-in-the-box pops out as one approaches the hostess stand.

Met Bar

London, England

SLEEK AND SWANK, MET BAR WAS DESIGNED AS A PRIVATE SANCTUARY FOR PROFESSIONALS IN THE CREATIVE MEDIA, OTHERWISE KNOWN AS THE "4M'S": MEDIA, MODELING, MOVIES, AND MUSIC. IT IS ALSO POPULAR WITH COSMOPOLITAN TRAVELERS STAYING IN THE ADJOINING METROPOLITAN HOTEL. DESIGNED AS A PRIVATE CLUB OPEN TO MEMBERS AND HOTEL RESIDENTS EXCLUSIVELY AFTER 6 P.M.,

the bar is accessible from the hotel lobby and from Old Park Lane. Although it is open for breakfast and serves as a public cafe throughout the day, the club shows its true colors after the sun goes down. That's when movers and shakers flock to the late-night lounge for cocktails, socializing, and dancing into the early morning hours. Designers chose materials that are shiny, reflective, and durable enough to endure the influx of dancers and revelers for long hours, seven days a week. Due to its A-list clientele, Met Bar evokes a sense of privacy and enclosure, reflected in a rich color

scheme of chocolate brown and cherry red, and subdued lighting throughout. A large, abstract mural of a New York cityscape lines the wall above the banquette. All furniture was specially commissioned for the bar, including cocktail tables with etched glass tops that reflect accent lighting. The mirrored end wall expands the interior and serves as a back-drop for the DJ booth. Glass rods are uplit to create a division between the DJ station and patrons. Dark brown Venetian polished plaster was used on the curvaceous walls to create depth, glamour and ambience.

architect: **Mark Pinney Associates** • interior designer: **United Designers**
square feet/meters: **1,995/185** • design budget: **not disclosed** • seats: **150**
photographers: **David Brittain; Tim Evans-Cook**

The alcove chairs, enclave booths, and round tables offer a sense of comfort and privacy. The hip and colorful cityscape along the back wall was inspired by the late Jean-Michel Basquiat. • Spaces are partitioned by uplit glass rods, combining form and function for a dramatic sculptured effect.

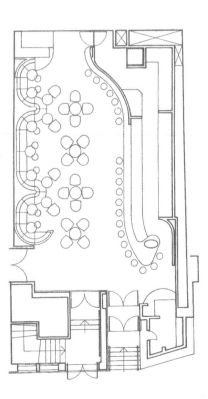

Hamiltons
Las Vegas, Nevada

ACTOR GEORGE HAMILTON IS KNOWN ABOUT TOWN FOR HIS PERENNIAL TAN AND AGELESS LOOKS. WHEN HE DECIDED TO OPEN HIS OWN PLACE, HE ASKED THE ARCHITECTS AND DESIGNERS TO VISUALIZE A SPACE THAT BROUGHT STYLE BACK TO GOING OUT. WITH HAMILTONS, LOCATED IN THE NEW YORK NEW YORK HOTEL, HAMILTON SUCCEEDED WITH AN UPSCALE LOUNGE AND CIGAR BAR THAT EXUDES

a distinctive Art Deco sensibility reminiscent of New York in the '30s. Using clean architectural lines and indirect cove lighting, the main room is a feast for the eyes. A coffered ceiling floats over the bar and plays against the striking period mural which is a montage of luxury liners and a metro cityscape. The geometric seating sits atop lush, leopard-print carpeting. And in the style of a jazz club, each table sports individual cafe lamps and ashtrays. The retro feel extends to the Steinway piano, mica wallpaper, and cobalt draperies. With the majestic New York skyline simulated by backlit photographic window panes, the resulting

ambience is sheer sophistication. The lounge has a terrace that overlooks the casino floor as well as a private party room, which is designed to look like the inside of a Pullman train car. The paneled walls and L-shaped seats contribute to the train motif, and a wall of windows allows patrons to spy the casino action below. From the outdoor perspective, the vast retail component is showcased with oversized windows that display extensive wares. Here, cigars and colorful retail displays are positioned for maximum exposure. In a clever move, the designers connected the retail store to the lounge though the walk-in humidor.

architect: David L. Downey Inc.
interior designers: O'Brien + Associates Design Inc. • George Hamilton Production • Desiderata
square feet/meters: 3,500/325 • design budget: $700,000 • seats: 80 • check average: $50
photographer: David Glomb

A full view into the smart and sophisticated site for cocktails, cigars, or a light bite. Leopard-print carpet, malachite bar top, stainless steel details, and a cove-lit dome enhance the sense of nostalgia. ● The glass-enclosed floor-to-ceiling humidor can be accessed from the retail store or the main lounge. It works as a bridge between the two rooms while serving as a display for the vast cigar selection. ● Inspired by the luxe railcars of the '30s, the private party room is set apart from the main space for special events. ● A wall of windows allows guests in the party room to watch the action in the casino below.

Hollywood Athletic Club
Hollywood, California

THE HOLLYWOOD ATHLETIC CLUB IS A TESTAMENT TO TINSELTOWN HISTORY. ORIGINALLY DESIGNED BY CECIL B. DE MILLE AND JOHN BARRYMORE, THE CLUB PLAYED HOST TO HOLLYWOOD ROYALTY IN ITS HEYDAY. IN 1997, DESIGNERS TRANSFORMED THE GYM INTO A LIVE MUSIC VENUE/NIGHTCLUB. TODAY, IT ATTRACTS A VARIED CROWD AND PERFORMERS FROM DAVID BOWIE TO FIONA APPLE.

The owner wanted the bar to make a grand statement at the entrance of the room. The wooden bar is rimmed with iron detailing that sets the pace for the 1920s Art Deco style with an abstract twist, created by oversized sconces and upended torchieres. Rich leather armchairs and sofas invite patrons to linger over drinks. Overhead, the original running track was transformed into the VIP gallery by replacing the sloped wooden

floor with one that is carpeted and level, providing a bird's-eye view of the stage. Below, the state-of-the-art dance floor and stage lighting signal show time. Decorative lighting, such as the oversized central pendant, is suspended so that it would not interfere with sight lines to the stage. For form and function, colorful drapery was used behind the stage and below the mezzanine to diffuse noise from the live musical acts.

Sound panels were also installed to absorb as much sound as possible. Other design challenges included adding an exit on the mezzanine level in accordance with building code and installing more washrooms for the anticipated influx of patrons. The only visible decorative element remaining from the original gym is the gleaming wood floor—the axis around which all the action pivots. The mezzanine, stage lighting, and scaffolding frame the upper level.

architect/interior designer: O'Brien + Associates Design Inc.
square feet/meters: 8,000/743 • design budget: $800,000 • seats: 450 • check average: $20
photographer: Paul Dennler

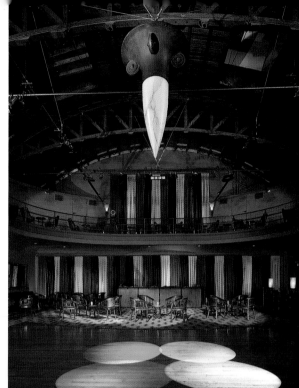

The first level is home to the main bar and lounge area, popular spots for a drink before the show begins. • The gargantuan pendant light provides a focal point to the massive dance floor and entertainment areas. The modernized lighting and sound systems facilitate the staging of big-name entertainers as well as dancing to a variety of musical styles.

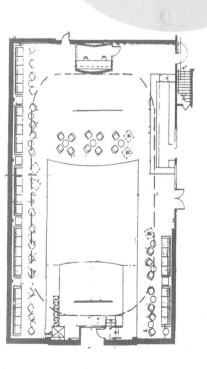

Tableaux Lounge
Tokyo, Japan

OVER-THE-TOP AND OOZING SOPHISTICATION, TABLEAUX LOUNGE ATTRACTS THE JAPANESE COSMOPOLITAN, THE INTERNATIONAL AVANT-GARDE, THE EXPATRIATE PROFESSIONAL, THE ENTERTAINMENT CELEBRITY, AND THE TRAVELER WHO SEEKS AN ELEGANT ENVIRONMENT. THE OWNER, WHO SET HIS SIGHTS ON THE CRÈME DE LA CRÈME, CLEARLY HAS ACHIEVED HIS GOAL. THE CONCEPT FOR TABLEAUX LOUNGE

is "chic elegance"—a place to relax with a premium cigar, a scotch, and other top-shelf pleasures. To obtain the sense of an exclusive retreat, the designer needed to overcome Tokyo's major architectural obstacle: lack of space. The odd configuration of structural ceiling beams, massive columns and angled walls left a tricky space to sculpt. By carving out multiple levels with distinct areas for socialization and privacy, the designer was able to maximize the effectiveness of the space. Ceiling heights of 9 feet to 13 feet further enhance the sense of expanse. Recalling the entertaining gallery in

a fine home, a piano is a central element, as are the fireplace, library, wine cellar, humidor, and bar. Lighting is another key element. Custom chandeliers, shaded wall sconces, and antique pendant fixtures are carefully placed to enhance the textures of the room. The subtle light plays well off the leathers, taffetas, leopard hides, brocades, fringes, dark woods, and crackle and gilded paint finishes. Mirrors and polished bar surfaces gleam, and plush red leather club chairs and banquettes punctuate the rooms with an air of masculine charm.

architects/interior designers: **O'Brien + Associates Design Inc.** • **Global Dining**
square feet/meters: 3,000/279 • design budget: $600,000 • seats: 60 • check average: $50
photographer: Atsushi Nakamichi

Chandeliers, sconces, and myriad fixtures reflect the gleaming floor, polished bar, and copper wall. • Expensive details transform the space into a mansion-like escape for the rich and famous. Rich leathers, plush brocades, and carved woods add panache at every turn. • The masculine bar is a showcase for the finer things in life. Wine racks, library books, humidors, and other luxe details connote elegance.

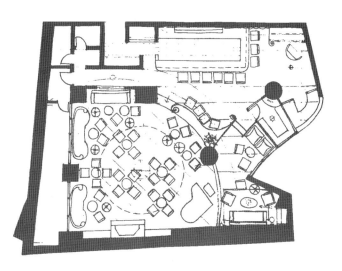

Stage Left
Maryland Heights, Missouri

COMBINING REFERENCES TO AMERICAN FILM AND THEATER WITH ICONOGRAPHY FROM ST. LOUIS HISTORY (THE WORLD'S FAIR AND CHARLES LINDBERGH'S PLANE, *THE SPIRIT OF ST. LOUIS*), STAGE LEFT IS A 7,300-SQUARE-FOOT VENUE DESIGNED TO RESEMBLE A HOLLYWOOD BACK LOT, WITH VARIOUS STAGE SETS, PROPS, AND ARTIFACTS. LIKE THE REST OF RIVERPORT CASINO, STAGE LEFT TARGETS SUBURBAN

St. Louis residents. Harrah's Entertainment and Players International initially commissioned Engstrom Design Group to create a lounge near the casino's waiting area. They came back with a proposal for a more dynamic venue, where patrons could eat, drink, and be entertained. Taking a high-energy stage-set approach to the space, designers convinced the clients to make the most of the site's challenging possibilities. To create the elaborate sets and props, a professional movie set fabricator was consulted. As patrons enter the theatrical venue, heavy draperies and floor treatments create the sense of walking on stage.

The bar is situated in front of the faux-brick set of an urban back alley, while the billiards room re-creates elements from *The Sting* and other popular films set in the gritty 1930s. A Victorian-era parlor, the rough-hewn porch, and 19th-century gazebo are raised gathering places where people can dine and take in the action. They are surrounded by old commercial building cutouts and an elevated "railway," which traverses the dining area. A dramatic color palette and highly patterned fabrics enhance the spirited atmosphere; a concept which is brought to life with the sound, music, and light of a multi-screen video system.

architect/interior designer: Engstrom Design Group
square feet/meters: 7,376/685 • design budget: $1.2 million • seats: 157 • check average: $10.00
photographer: Hank Young

The vaulted industrial ceilings, neon lights, awnings, street scenes and elevated "railway" all suggest the pleasures of a lively outdoor - fairgrounds or Hollywood production set. • Although patrons are actually inside, they can enjoy drinks from the vantage point of an open-air gazebo. The lifted gazebo allows patrons to look out on all the action below.

Bunker
Napoli, Italy

BUNKER REPRESENTS THE FIFTH ATTEMPT TO ESTABLISH A SUCCESSFUL NIGHTCLUB IN THE MASSIVE, RAMBLING SPACE THAT IS NOW AN ULTRA-HOT NIGHTSPOT. THIS TIME, THE ACE TEAM AT GNOSIS ARCHITETTURA USED THE NATURAL UNDERGROUND AREA TO THEIR ADVANTAGE. AS THE NAME SUGGESTS, BUNKER IS A SUB-LEVEL STRUCTURE, MUCH LIKE A FORTRESS. PATRONS DESCEND A SERIES OF STAIRS TO ENTER THE

edifice, which incorporates a series of service bars, lounge areas, and a massive space for dancing. The architects capitalized on the theme of caves and their natural stratification to create the sensation that one is floating through a maze of water-filled, underground caverns. Ethereal blue light plays a major role in creating an otherworldly, aquatic sensibility. Stepping down the "liquid" staircase, patrons feel as though they are literally coasting on a fluorescent wave. The blue lights on the main dance floor are designed to evoke the sense of movement abreast an

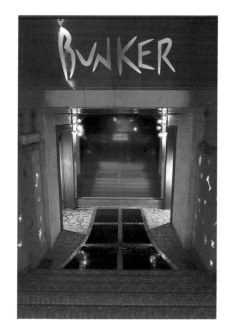

undulating blue lake. Fragmented stonework on the floors and bright white perimetral bar islands are intended to recall the colors, textures, and imagery of the ancient city of Cumae. The white stucco bars are spattered with multicolored textural fragments, and are topped in Bunker's signature azure. The large central dance floor makes use of a sophisticated lighting system to animate the space. Technological advances are evident in the sound system as well—an integral component of the club's success as one of the most popular dancing spots in Napoli.

architect: Gnosis Architettura
square feet/meters: 13,423/1,247 • design budget: $300,000 • seats: 350 • check average: $15
photographers: Piero De Simone; Francesco Rotili

The blinding white stucco structures found on many Mediterranean islands inspired the bar stations. • Changing blue lights on the disco floor and throughout reinforce the pervasive aquatic theme. Overhead, an advanced lighting system creates mystery and changing scenery in time with the music. • The fragmented stone flooring re-creates the ambience of the rambling corridors of a mystical seaside town.

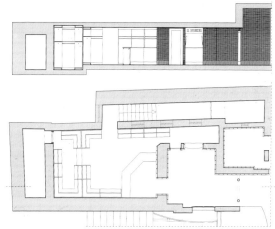

The Garden of Eden

Hollywood, California

THE GARDEN OF EARTHLY DELIGHTS WAS THE CONCEPT FOR THIS NIGHTSPOT DESIGNED TO TEMPT THE 20-35-YEAR-OLD CROWD, AND PROMPT THEM TO EXPERIENCE THE NIGHT IN DOWNTOWN HOLLYWOOD. OWNER DAVID JUDAKEN SET HIS SIGHTS ON A RUN-DOWN HIGH-RISE IN A SKETCHY POCKET OF HOLLYWOOD. HE CALLED UPON THE EXPERTISE OF O'BRIEN + ASSOCIATES TO CONJURE UP THE HEADY

and exotic feeling evocative of Morocco; the ambience that prevails in ancient cities such as Marrakech and Casablanca. O'Brien and Judaken journeyed to Morocco in search of inspiration and authentic goods with which to outfit the club. They picked up exotic raw metal lanterns, colorful silk, tile, fabric, ceramics, and an array of paraphernalia that would suit the theme. Meanwhile, the construction team back in the States grappled with the creation of a multilevel venue. To achieve the raised lounge, the upper level VIP area and the elevated seating around the dance floor required an aggressive construction plan, with the

use of thousands of pounds of steel. Designers created a sweeping, curved staircase which leads to the VIP lounge and allows views to virtually all points in the club below. A skilled craftsman fashioned fantastical wood carvings throughout. Handmade mirrors and antique doors open onto the main floor lounge, where wood forms, domed soffits, and arches define the architecture. Patrons can stop by the dance floor, or go up to the chic, raised lounge to sit in massive stuffed chairs beside a raging fireplace. An ornate chandelier hangs from the domed ceiling and lights the grand bar framed with Moroccan carvings.

architects: O'Brien + Associates Design Inc. • Stan Brent • interior designer: O'Brien + Associates Design Inc.
square feet/meters: 9,000/836 • design budget: $1.35 million • seats: 150 • check average: $30
photographer: David Glomb

Using temple-shaped soffits, hanging Moroccan lanterns, and inlaid wood detailing, the designer created an ancient, authentic aura in the bar area. The harem-like quality of the lounge/bar area is accented with lush draperies and overstuffed chairs. • The multilevel design allows patrons to enjoy the privacy of a lush, Arabian-style seating nook while at the same time viewing the action just a few steps below. The use of scrolled iron railing provides an intricate focal point while leaving views unobstructed. • The polished wood floors gleam, but the eye is immediately drawn to the marvelous wooden inlaid ceiling, peak-shaped soffits, and magical drapery, which evoke exotic drama. • Hand-painted decorative art, colorized finishes, and inspired custom lighting create a fantasy for the bar patron. • Infusing one corner with a pop art sensibility, an over-sized Marilyn Monroe mural is juxtaposed against the Moroccan motif. Keyhole cutouts in the wall allow extra light, and add visual interest.

Chart House
Tokyo Bay, Japan

THE HOTEL INTER-CONTINENTAL TOKYO BAY IS IDEALLY SITUATED IN THE EPICENTER OF THE CITY'S NEW WATERFRONT AREA—A THRIVING HUB OF COMMERCE AND TOURISM. INSIDE THE ELEGANT HOTEL ARE A PLUSH ANTEROOM AS WELL AS A LOUNGE DESIGNED TO ATTRACT GUESTS OF THE ADJOINING RESTAURANT BEFORE AND AFTER MEALS. BOTH ARE ALSO POPULAR WITH HOTEL GUESTS AND VISITORS

who stop in for cocktails in extremely highbrow surroundings that boast an unparalleled view. The setting practically oozes refinement, sophistication, and European charm. Highly polished dark wood accents frame the bar, wall moldings, built-in liquor display cabinets, and furnishings. An uplit, coffered ceiling serves to open the room visually as it imparts a warm glow above table groupings. In the bar section, richly upholstered sofas and clubby chairs provide a welcome respite from a hectic business meeting or day of sightseeing. The overall effect is a bar with a decidedly European flair.

The lobby, on the other hand, uses a wall of plate glass windows to show off the stunning vistas of Tokyo Bay. At night, the lights of the city and particularly of the bridge, create a magical effect. A cerulean ceiling painting, complete with azure sky and cumulus clouds completes the illusion of being able to reach out and touch the world outside the window. To entice patrons to relax and linger, a grand piano is set up in the midst of the viewing areas. When the sun sets, the enchanting spot is generally bustling with an energetic mix of tourists and hotel guests.

architect: **Nihon Sekkei, Inc.** • interior designer: **Hirsch-Bedner Associates**
square feet/meters: 969/90 • design budget: $193,800 • seats: 34
photographer: **Jaime Ardiles-Arce**

The lounge area features floor-to-ceiling windows for wraparound views. ● The decor is tied together with elegant appointments, including custom furnishings, upholstery, and lighting. Highly polished wood accents can be found on tables, chairs, the bar, and framing the liquor displays.

MacArthur's

Atlanta, Georgia

THE DESIGN PROJECT FOR MACARTHUR'S WAS DEMANDING BECAUSE THE SITE WAS ORIGINALLY CREATED AS A PROTOTYPICAL FAST-FOOD RESTAURANT, COMPLETE WITH DRIVE-THROUGH FACILITIES. CONSTRUCTION WAS UNDERWAY WHEN THE OWNER DECIDED TO ALTER THE CONCEPT TO AN UPSCALE, FULL-SERVICE BAR AND RESTAURANT. SEIBER DESIGN MET THE CHALLENGE BY ALTERING THE FENESTRATION,

stripping off telltale fast-food details, adding the curving bar, and installing the unusual tower structure. Following the owners' vision of a private club atmosphere that departed from the traditional dimly lit mens' club, the concept appeals to both men and women and provides a contemporary setting that complements original artwork. Maintaining a simple materials palette, the designers included brick, stucco and metal on the exterior, and stained concrete, maple veneer, painted gypsum board, and exposed structural steel on the interior. Streamlined,

curving surfaces and planes contrast with rectilinear elements, such as the steel-clad tower roof, the standing seam metal bar roof, and the curving brick wall leading in from Peachtree Street. Inside, the exposed steel columns are reflected in the graphic patterns of the booth fabric and wood trim. Reflected in the table lamps is the round shape of pendant lights hanging over the bar. The glass and steel piano lounge tower, designed to simulate a gas lantern inside and out, affords views outdoors and is a stylish point of interest for passersby.

architect/interior designer: Seiber Design, Inc.
square feet/meters: 4,500/418 • design budget: $846,000 • seats: 160 • check average: $30
photographer: Dot Griffith

Simplicity is the watchword, creating spare, modern silhouettes. The gently curving bar is mirrored by a curved soffit above. A set of track lights shines on the liquor selections, while more decorative - pendant lights dangle from the soffit. • The piano lounge is punctuated by a series of small groupings near the bar where soft candlelight is the only illumination required. • A frontal view of the bar shows off the spartan materials palette of stainless steel accents and wooden finishes on bar stools, shelving, and ceiling details.

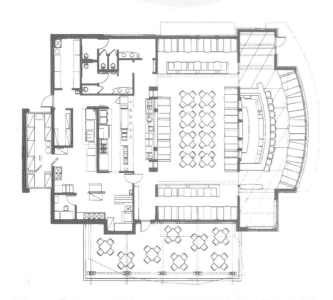

The Wave

London, Ontario

THE WAVE REPLACED AN INSTITUTIONALLY BARREN AND INFLEXIBLE DANCE CLUB ON THE UNIVERSITY OF WESTERN ONTARIO CAMPUS. THE PRIMARY OBJECTIVE WAS TO REPOSITION THE MASSIVE SPACE FROM ITS FORMER ROLE AS "TECHNO" NIGHTCLUB INTO A VENUE WITH MULTIFARIOUS USES—RESTAURANT, PUB, DANCE HALL, LIVE ENTERTAINMENT SPOT, AND A PLACE TO ESCAPE FROM THE PRESSURE OF EXAMS.

The first step in transforming the existing structure was to break down the cold space into warmer, more human dimensions. The architects achieved this by scaling the room into smaller areas, then infusing the decor with a tropical theme. The newly designed oasis is accented with crocodile and flamingo carvings on the rafters, tropical cutouts on booth dividers, and multicolored fish and animal designs carved into the linoleum floor. Photographs of graduating classes, sports teams, and other university memorabilia evoke good times at the school. Patron comfort and spatial distinctions were achieved with the addition of

booths and benches. Increased service and merchandising was added with a new beer and shooter hut as well as visually appealing hot and cold food bars. Instead of guessing what the young audience wanted, designers consulted the student council, which provided valuable input critical to the successful redesign. The designers brightened up the existing industrial elements with vibrant paint and custom lighting. Easily vandalized drywall surfaces were replaced with particle board or galvanized metal. The existing furniture was reconfigured to allow group seating, and reupholstered to maximize comfort. The oasis was complete.

architect: Malholtra Nicholson Architects • interior designer: Cricket Design Company Inc.
square feet/meters: 9,000/836 • design budget: $270,000 • seats: 680 • check average: $15
photographer: Richard Johnson, Interior Images

The portico-like bar was brought close to the entrance to create a sense of arrival and to allow easier service and patron traffic. • Simulating a beach hut, this seating area effectively breaks down the space, creates comfortable dining alcoves, and repeats the tropical beach party theme. • The industrial look was preserved yet brightened considerably with a few coats of vibrant, tropical paint, creative lighting, and user-friendly bar stations. • Because the former wooden dance floor was expensive to maintain and exposed to excessive wear and tear, the designers replaced it with durable linoleum, adding a splash of style and color.

Monsoon Cafe
Santa Monica, California

SINCE THE DESIGNER SET OUT TO CRAFT A ROUGH-HEWN SPACE WITH ASIAN UNDERCURRENTS, MONSOON IS NOT SLICK AND POLISHED, BUT RATHER CASUAL AND EXOTIC. COMBINING VARIED MATERIALS INDIGENOUS TO SOUTHEAST ASIA, THE AMBIENCE TAKES PATRONS ON A MYSTICAL JOURNEY. THE WORD "MONSOON" CONJURES UP AN ARRAY OF TROPICAL IMAGES AND FEELINGS. THE RESTAURANT PLAYS

on the sensory cues in a whirlwind of visual, musical, and culinary elements from Southeast Asia. The first-floor cocktail bar is a stopping point where patrons can take in the sights and a light bite before dinner. Inlaid pearl and ebony stone and glazed concrete floors simulate a rain washed surface. Diners are then escorted to their tables in the main dining room—a theater of dining. The huge open exhibition kitchen is the focal point of the space. Other sightlines offer a wealth of visual stimuli, such as a giant chandelier, complementary smaller fixtures, bamboo-clad mezzanine structures, and

tropical plantings that exude Indonesian flavor. The lighting was created by a Tokyo artist who incorporated the Asian motif with cast bronze dragon heads, jeweled and beaded ornamentation, and festive blown-glass lights. Hand-carved bamboo panels, brocades, and textural furnishings reinforce the theme. In the main bar and live music lounge upstairs, patrons can enjoy dancing, cocktails, and a light menu of Asian specialties. In order to increase the space in the lounge, the ceiling truss was removed and the roof suspended from a steel beam, effectively tripling the size of the room.

architect/interior designer: O'Brien + Associates Design Inc.
square feet/meters: 12,500/1,161 • design budget: $2 million • seats: 200 • check average: $25
photographer: David Glomb

The bar's carved wood trellis, bamboo furnishings, custom light fixtures, and native Asian decorative elements set the tone for the restaurant's exotic cuisine. • The upstairs lounge is a gathering spot for live music, cocktails, and light dining. The beaded curtain creates a feeling of mystery upon entering the second-floor space. The low coffee tables and lounge furnishings, including benches, armoires, and artifacts, are from Indonesia and the Philippines. • The two-story space features native Southeast Asian masks and decorative objects.

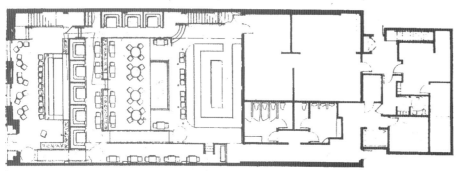

Churchill Bar
London, England

WHEN IT COMES TO ENTERTAINING WITH CLASSIC ELEGANCE, THE BRITISH CERTAINLY KNOW HOW TO KEEP THE TENETS OF YESTERYEAR ALIVE. PERHAPS IT'S THEIR PROXIMITY TO THE ROYAL FAMILY AND BUCKINGHAM PALACE THAT HAS HELPED THE BRITISH RETAIN THE UNCANNY ABILITY TO IMBUE THEIR DESIGNS WITH STATELY CHARM. THE DESIGN OF CHURCHILL BAR, FOR EXAMPLE, EMBODIES THE AURA OF

an exclusive men's club while attracing a sophisticated contemporary clientele. The bar reflects the era embodied by Sir Winston Churchill in an atmosphere incorporating authentic accessories from a historic collection. The masculine restaurant serves eclectic international brasserie-style cuisine, with updated influences. The overriding tone of the space is one of distinction and elegance. Walls, ceiling, and bar are all embellished with dark

mahogany paneling, polished to a high sheen. The bar itself is topped in strong marble. A wall display of crystal decanters illuminates the vast selection of premium liquors. Adjacent to the bar, expensive upholstered seating groupings are carefully arranged atop deep burgundy Oriental carpets in a setting that comes alive with piano music. These intimate groupings, plush furnishings, and soft lighting details combine to create a venue that is at once inviting and impressive. Toward the back wall, a venerable lit display case discreetly houses authentic Churchill memorabilia. Books, photos, and personal effects are arranged with a personal touch. In fact, in this area, it is possible to imagine that one is lounging in a private home rather than a public space. The restaurant features tables topped in crisp white linens. The expansive room is framed by a wall of windows, swathed in custom drapery that manages to shield patrons from the busy road outside.

interior designer: Hirsch-Bedner Associates
square feet/meters: 1,300/121 • design budget: $169,000 • seats: 56
photographer: Alex Brattel

The masculine bar is at once stately and inviting, discretely punctuated with authentic Churchill memorabilia. The dark wood paneling and crystal decanters showcase the bar's extensive selection of premium spirits. • The large restaurant is a study in elegant simplicity. Austere white linens top each table, and the ceiling is punctuated with unobtrusive pin lights that cast a soft glow on the tables below.

Southend Brewery & Smokehouse
Charlotte, North Carolina

THE CHALLENGE: TAKE A MASSIVE, NONDESCRIPT '30s-ERA WAREHOUSE IN A BLIGHTED AREA OF DOWNTOWN'S SOUTH END, AND TURN IT INTO A SUCCESSFUL NIGHTSPOT. WHERE TO BEGIN? FIRST, DESIGNERS SET ABOUT SCALING THE IMMENSE, TWO-STORY RESTAURANT TO A MORE APPROACHABLE 14,000-SQUARE-FOOT RESTAURANT AND BAR. NEXT, ATTRACT A BROAD SPECTRUM OF PATRONS TO

a less than desirable part of town. The solution: accentuate the raw beauty of the structure with graphic signage and create a convivial atmosphere. The design team played up the exposed structural and engineering systems, planning around beams, columns, fixtures, even obsolete plumbing equipment. The industrial components are contrasted by a sophisticated dining experience on one side and a more lively bar and outdoor patio on the other. The focal point is the glass encased brewhouse, functional yet beautiful in its simplicity and translucency. Secondary design elements include a wood-burn-

ing pizza oven encircled by a bar, and a sculptural steel staircase. Attractive signage, custom lighting, and see-and-be-seen seating create visual excitement. The pizza bar and kitchen are both exposed to heighten Southend's entertainment value and to carry the sights and smells of cooking into the dining area. The faux-finished pizza bar attracts single diners who can enjoy a bite and conversation while the main bar offers a view of the interior space as well as the patio. The bar's hanging light fixtures, which are more fluid and organic in design, bridge the interior and exterior areas.

architect: Shook Design Group, Inc. • interior designer: Hixson Design
square feet/meters: 14,000/1,300 • design budget: $1.2 million • seats: 350 • check average: $26
photographer: Tim Buchman

The signage and graphic elements were designed to celebrate the industrial age of the '30s and '40s. The metal grain silo is emblazoned with the colorful period logo, which draws passersby and establishes brand recognition. • The glass encased brewhouse is surrounded by points of interest such as the theatrical staircase leading to the mezzanine.

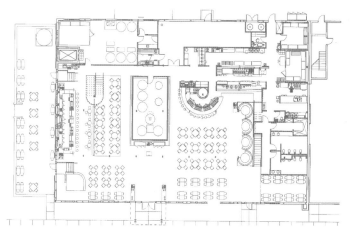

Bar Tiepolo
Venice, Italy

WHEN PRODUCING A VENUE IN ONE OF THE MOST BEAUTIFUL, HISTORIC, AND ROMANTIC CITIES IN THE WORLD, ARCHITECTS AND DESIGNERS KNOW IT WOULD BE FOOLISH TO COUNTER THE NATURAL ORDER OF THAT SETTING. THE CREATORS OF BAR TIEPOLO WERE SMART ENOUGH TO KNOW THEY HAD A GEM ON THEIR HANDS WHEN THEY WERE ASKED TO RE-DESIGN THE STATELY BAR IN THE FORMER TIEPOLO

Palazzo on the Grand Canal in Venice. According to the owner's wishes, the design team set out to return the interior of this 16th-century Venetian style palazzo to its former grandeur in the Hotel Europa & Regina. The intent was to position the bar at the main artery of the public areas to attract both tourists and local residents with a taste for the finer things in life. Since Venice is notorious for its debilitating floods, the design team chose elegant yet indestructible marble for the floors and the lower portion of the walls. Higher up, where water damage is not a concern, gilded quilted leather panels were introduced above the

wainscot to add a sense of luxury and warmth. To camouflage unsightly lighting and mechanical details, designers discreetly concealed wiring within the handsome wood beam ceiling.

To further enhance the elegance of the room, the appointments are embellished in a rich palette of golden brocade, silk, and gilded wood. And of course, since the hotel is in one of Italy's most alluring destination cities, what room would be finished without art? Gargoyle sculptures, framed oil prints, and carved moldings all speak of fine craftsmanship. The art is illuminated with professional attention, indulging the eye in a visual feast.

architect: Giancarlo Brusati • interior designer: Hirsch-Bedner Associates
square feet/meters: 750/70 • design budget: $225,000 • seats: 32
photographer: Jaime Ardiles-Arce

127

Sculptures and oil prints reflect the
history of Venice and top off the bar's
luxe details. • A functional component
to the room is its hidden infrastructure.
All wiring and electrical elements are
discreetly tucked out of view, hidden
in the wooden beamed ceiling.

Big Shots
Dallas, Texas

WHEN WE THINK OF A SPORTS BAR OR A POOL HALL, THE LAST IMAGE THAT COMES TO MIND IS ONE OF SOPHISTICATION. NONETHELESS, BIG SHOTS MANAGES TO TAKE THESE HERETOFORE GRITTY, "MASCULINE" CONCEPTS TO NEW HEIGHTS OF ELEGANCE. THE STYLISH, CONTEMPORARY DECOR SERVES AS A HIP BACKDROP FOR A HOST OF ACTIVITIES—COCKTAILS, A LIGHT BITE, DINNER, A

game of pool, a fine cigar. The designer's goal was to create a contemporary, fun environment, while making a connection to historical precedence, particularly in regard to the pool hall. Of great concern was lighting over the pool tables. The clients, who have many years of experience in the pool hall business, had very specific require ments for the type of light, the distance from the table, and the spacing of the lights. Instead of placing three fixtures over the table, the area was simplified with large, rectangular white canvas shades that surround the fixtures. Another clever element of the design is the use of

sensuously shaped and boldly colored booths. In addition to adding a great deal of character and style to the bar, the booths are removable. When today's bold contemporary look becomes tomorrow's out-of-style fashion, or when the booths show signs of wear, they can be replaced to breathe new life into the venue without gutting the existing design. Another challenge was how to serve food in the pool area itself which only allowed for a 5-inch-deep drink rail along the walls. The ingenious solution was loosely based on the trays that hooked to car windows at the drive-ins of the 1950s.

interior designer: **Paul Draper and Associates, Inc.**
square feet/meters: 7,500/697 • design budget: not disclosed • seats: 126
photographer: Richard Klein

An impressive array of mahogany pool tables gives a nod to the pool halls of days gone by. Mod stools line the pool hall—a perfect place to sit with a scotch before picking up a pool cue. Custom lighting bathes each table in a glare-free glow. • Pendant lights illuminate the dining area and show off the boldly colored booths, tucked away TV screens, and polished wooden walls. • Big screen viewing areas draped with curtains, multiple seating options, and vibrantly colored booths add a dash of depth to the pared-down dining room.

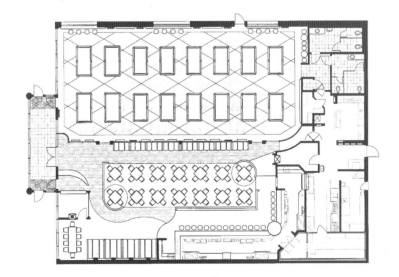

Superior
Toronto, Ontario

THE GOAL WAS TO TAKE A 117-YEAR-OLD BUILDING THAT HAD SUFFERED THROUGH VARIOUS INCARNATIONS AND TRANSFORM IT TO RESEMBLE ITS ORIGINAL NAMESAKE, UPDATING THE SPACE WITH MODERN DETAILS IN ORDER TO ATTRACT A WIDE CLIENTELE. WHEN THE ORIGINAL OWNER'S GRANDSONS STEPPED IN, THEY INFUSED THE VACANT SPACE WITH A COLORFUL, HIP, '90s LOOK WHILE RESPECTING THE

original structure. The entrance was designed as a frameless glass structure, so the impact of the unique building hits passersby immediately. Located on the longest street in Canada (that is currently undergoing a major revitalization program), Superior is a contemporary interpretation of traditional style. This was expressed with the use of aged finishes and sturdy materials, including wood, brick and wrought iron. The second floor was cut back to follow the natural curve of the bar and enable upstairs patrons to look down on the happenings below. The bar top itself is crafted of two different

finishes: wood and marble. Each has a different height, but both encourage patrons to enjoy the fresh oysters being shucked in full view. The original roof's framing joists and dormers were exposed during the removal of the third floor and construction of the mezzanine level. The resulting spectacular 40-foot ceiling continues to dazzle first-time customers. The exposed brick walls and checkerboard flooring are also original features that not only add character but function well today. Vividly colored pendant lights provide a dash of color and fun.

interior designer: Hirschberg Design Group Ltd.
square feet/meters: 3,850/358 • design budget: $241,000 • seats: 145 • check average: $12
photographer: Richard Johnson, Interior Images

Although the exposed rafters and brick wall create a grand scale, the addition of a mezzanine level provides a cozy spot for booths underneath. • The bar was designed to encourage patrons to sit and enjoy something to eat along with their drinks. An enticing array of fresh seafood. is offered at the oyster pan. Adding points of color are vibrant hanging pendant lights.

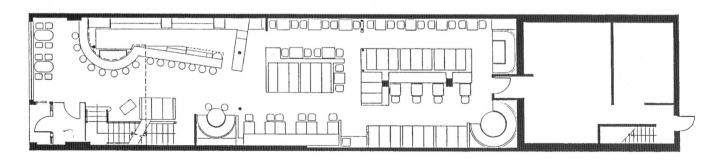

Payard Patisserie and Bistro
New York, New York

IN NEW YORK CITY, DANIEL BOULUD, OWNER OF THE FAMED RESTAURANT DANIEL, HAS THE MIDAS TOUCH. SO WHEN HIS PASTRY CHEF FRANCOIS PAYARD YEARNED FOR A PLACE OF HIS OWN, BOULUD MADE HIM A BETTER OFFER. TODAY, THE TWO ARE PARTNERS IN PAYARD PATISSERIE AND BISTRO, A WELCOME ADDITION TO MANHATTAN'S UPPER EAST SIDE AND AN INSTANT HIT WITH "THE LADIES WHO

lunch." Crucial to the success of such a venture is the interior design. The team sought out the Rockwell Group for the task, asking David Rockwell to re-create an old-world ambience that would impart a sense of Paris' Left Bank to Lexington Avenue. The concept incorporated a European-style bistro and patisserie, serving pastries as well as more substantial food from early morning to late evening. The first challenge was to unify the bakery and the bistro and create a sense of progression from one space to the next. The task was accomplished by placing the baked goods in appealing glass cases along the perimeter of one side, and erecting an open bar

complete with wine racks on the other. Customers enter through the patisserie doors, where a mosaic floor is inset with whimsical motifs of coffee cups, croissants, and baguettes. Custom glass and mahogany cases display a tempting array of Payard's signature sweets. Creamy painted plaster walls and intricate ceiling frieze set off the wood and marble for a spacious, classical effect. A cluster of tables surrounds the center columns, which are mounted with a custom-blown glass lighting fixture inspired by chef's whisks. A curving bar and paneled mahogany partitions flank the open portal to the two-level bistro dining space just beyond.

architect/interior designer: **Rockwell Group**
square feet/meters: **7,000/650** • design budget: not disclosed • seats: **100**
photographer: © Paul Warchol

Whimsical lighting fixtures fastened to the massive structural columns define the space. The bistro's dark wood floor contrasts against the more casual custom tile in the patisserie. • Patrons can enjoy an early morning espresso, late-night cocktails at the back bar, and more hearty fare in the two-story main bistro.

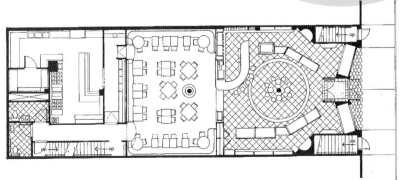

Carrot's Cafe
Rome, Italy

THIS IS A SMALL WINE AND BEER BAR AIMED AT ITALY'S YOUNGER GENERATION. AS SUCH, THE DESIGN FOCUS IS DECIDEDLY CASUAL, EMPLOYING AN ARRAY OF INDUSTRIAL MATERIALS IN A WHIMSICAL FASHION TO CREATE A RELAXED PLACE TO ENJOY A GLASS OF WINE OR BEER WITHOUT AIRS. THE MAIN BAR IS SET AGAINST AN EXPOSED BRICK WALL. ALL THE ORIGINAL PLUMBING AND FIXTURING IS VISIBLE TO

create a sense of connectedness with the space. The bar itself is an example of what can be achieved when both budget and space are limited. Everything is exposed for the patrons to see, even the keg barrels. Clearly, the industrial steel facade indicates that the designers decided to have fun with simple commercial materials. The concept was to create a cutting-edge work rather than a traditional pub. The use of wood and brick represents perhaps the interior's only link with tradition. Marking the venue's thrust toward

the future are railings, steel facades on the furnishings, and a spiral staircase. Another facet of the contemporary appeal is the neon lighting, employed not only to cast a colorful glow against the walls and exposed pipes, but also to attract passersby. The industrial motif is extended through a color palette that is decidedly neutral, except for periodic infusions of cobalt. The result is an informal hangout where patrons can linger over a beer, watch a game on TV with friends, or sample a diverse selection of wines.

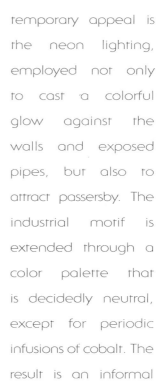

architect/interior designer: Ciccotti Arredamenti Negozi s.r.l.
square feet/meters: 969/90 • design budget: $130,950 • seats: 60 • check average: $12
photographer: Francesca Francisi

Much of the appeal of the space is that it feels like a funky version of a friend's basement. The industrial details and concrete flooring let patrons know that this is a gathering spot that doesn't stand on ceremony. • To maximize use of the small space, designers built a simple banquette system along one wall. • The spartan furnishings employ soft leather cushions atop steel bases. The "carrot" stools add a dash of whimsy, and are easily moved for impromptu get-togethers with friends at nearby tables.

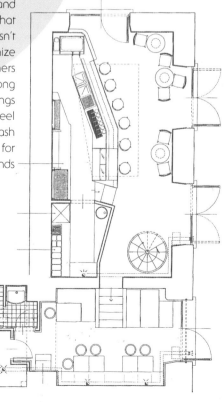

ZuZu's Coffee Bar
Hartford, Connecticut

SERVING COFFEE BY DAY AND COCKTAILS BY NIGHT, ZUZU'S MAKES THE MOST OF ITS QUIRKY ARTS AND CRAFTS STOREFRONT LOCATION ACROSS THE STREET FROM THE HARTFORD CIVIC CENTER. THE ORIGINAL SPACE WAS HOME TO A FLOWER SHOP AND A SHOE STORE BUILT AT THE TURN OF THE CENTURY. AS HISTORY WOULD HAVE IT, THE BUILDING EXUDES TREMENDOUS INHERENT CHARM, WHICH THE

designers wisely chose to embellish. Some of its high points: a double-height space with floor-to-ceiling glass, arched entryways, a weathered terra-cotta floor, custom oak stairway and mezzanine, and meticulous faux timbered ceiling. In keeping with its original character, the architects altered very little on the main level and concentrated on finishes, furniture, fixtures, and cabinetwork. Walls were sponge painted in a warm ochre set off by customized light fixtures. To furnish the space, the designers scavenged Hudson Valley antique

stores for funky Victorian pieces, such as settees, scroll arm divans, and high-backed armchairs. The focal point of the lively space is the dark stained oak bar, with inset paneling and rope molding trim. The back bar lies flat against the wall, while the front bar wraps around existing columns in a sensuous curve. The cellar, originally slated as office, storage, and bathroom space, is now used for extra seating. Outfitted with a vinyl harlequin floor pattern and soft colors, it doubles as a gallery for local artists, and a hide-away for more intimate conversation.

architect: Rosenberg Kolb Architects, PC
square feet/meters: 2,500/232 • design budget: $500,000
photographer: Jan Staller

The terra-cotta floor, stained oak bar, and two-story layout create an enticing lounge atmosphere. • Hand-picked flea market finds and Victorian pieces create comfortable seating on the mezzanine.

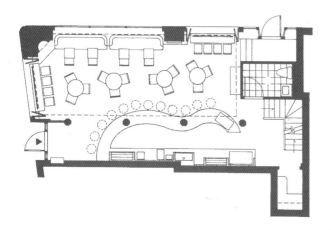

Rave
New York, New York

CREATED ON A SHOESTRING BUDGET IN THE HEART OF TIMES SQUARE, RAVE WAS DESIGNED TO TRIPLE AS A LUNCH CAFE/BAR FOR THE LOCAL FASHION AVENUE CLIENTELE, AN AFTER-WORK GATHERING SPOT, AND A LATE-NIGHT BAR THAT WOULD DRAW PATRONS LEAVING THE BUSY NIGHTCLUB ACROSS THE STREET. THE THEME IS A '90s VERSION OF A DINER, WITH INTERIORS WHICH FEATURE CLEAN LINES, BOLD

shapes, neon, and an unobstructed view of the central bar. The designer expended the majority of the budget on the two items that would be touched most often. First, a bar top of avonite was created with a thick radius edge and hand-polished luster. The second move was to incorporate interesting upholstery fabrics such as pony skin tabletops—a smart choice since most of the clientele is in the garment industry. Using simple materials in a fresh way, the designer transformed the pole from a chain-link fence into a floating bolster on the banquette; the seat is plywood wrapped in foam. The exposed brick walls are painted a creamy yellow

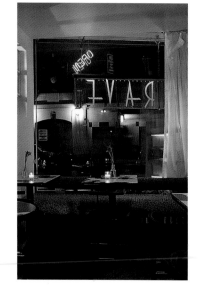

set off with an intense chalk blue while the back wall glows with a simple fluorescent light fixture. At the center of the room, waves of blue laminate make up the bar facade. The top is separated from the base by clear acrylic spheres that create a floating effect. In the bar's center is a clock flanked by glass shelving. Glass panels with neon art are also used to visually separate the room. One panel depicts Atlas with the weight of the world on his shoulders; the other, an Art Deco-style woman reaching for da Vinci's *Perfect Man*. The floor's blue and white stripes lend a dynamic touch and create the illusion of additional width.

interior designer: Burbidge design/construction
square feet/meters: 1,600/149 • design budget: $50,000 • seats: 75
photographer: © image/dennis krukowski

The main architectural challenge was the long and narrow proportions of the room. Using stripes of blue and white vinyl, the designer created the illusion of added width. The glass panels with neon art serve as creative partitions. Creamy yellow walls are softly lit, and upholstery is executed in luxe textured fabric. ● The back of the bar features an oversized clock with Roman numerals, flanked by glass shelves lit with neon rods.

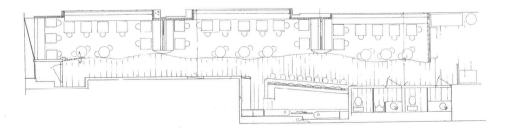

Bitter End B Side
Austin, Texas

THE DESIGN OBJECTIVE FOR BITTER END B SIDE WAS TO PRESERVE THE INDUSTRIAL CHARACTER OF THE EXISTING WAREHOUSE WHILE PROVIDING AN EXCITING VENUE FOR LIVE MUSIC AND OVERFLOW SPACE FOR THE ADJOINING RESTAURANT. SINCE THE RESTAURANT WAS ALREADY IN EXISTENCE, THE ARCHITECTS RESPECTED THE DESIGN AND COLOR PALETTE THAT WAS PREVIOUSLY ESTABLISHED. THE EXTREMELY

high warehouse ceilings are in keeping with the open structure of the building and exude a feeling of expanse. A predominant, massive, exposed brick wall, further reinforces an industrial look. The brick theme is extended in structural columns as well as table legs. Additional materials include concrete and wood in the ceiling. The mezzanine houses a small stage, where live bands can play without infringing on the space. It is used for drinking, dancing, and socializing, with a series of casual seating arrangements

lined along the bar and scattered throughout. All sport mica-topped tables for easy cleanup, surrounded by simple bar stools upholstered in vibrant yellow.

Color accents used along the staircase and balcony are emblazoned in bold red—the infusions of color in an otherwise natural color scheme. The lighting effects are created by custom hanging pendants. As a live music venue, special attention was paid to the electronic effects, including a state-of-the-art sound system with great acoustics.

architect/interior designer: Dick Clark Architecture
square feet/meters: 2,700/251 • design budget: $270,000 • seats: 100 • check average: $20
photographer: Paul Bardagjy

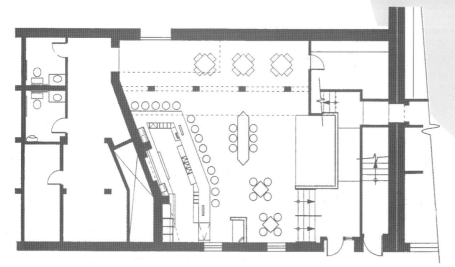

The massive warehouse structure is framed by the central backdrop: a floor-to-ceiling exposed brick wall, which houses the main bar. • The architect made the most of the high ceilings by installing a mezzanine level with a space to host live musical acts. • The abundance of seating choices allows for light dining and cocktails, as well as numerous vantage points.

ZaZa

Toronto, Ontario

AFTER OPERATING SUCCESSFUL RESTAURANTS AND BARS IN TORONTO'S SUBURBS, THE OWNERS OF ZAZA SET OUT TO CREATE A NEW DOWNTOWN VENTURE THAT WOULD EPITOMIZE THE DINING TRENDS OF THE FUTURE. WORKING WITH THE INNOVATORS AT II BY IV DESIGN ASSOCIATES, THEY CREATED A SPACE THEY DESCRIBE AS "FRANK LLOYD WRIGHT MEETS THE '90s." THE OWNERS' GOAL WAS

to create a "people place"—a comfortable surrounding for residents and visitors alike. The long empty commercial building with forbidding stainless steel front and raw concrete interior presented the greatest challenge, next to the need to compete with two restaurants on either side. The designers met the challenges by removing the entire facade of the building and installing custom garage doors. Cold granite and steel finishes were replaced with wood, stucco, and natural slate. The result is a welcoming exterior that seems to have no boundaries. The interior is comfortable and spacious with minimal

architectural detailing—modern materials and lighting effects add personality. A trio of bars (espresso, seafood and antipasto) grace the front area, which is flanked by drink stations; a sleek cocktail lounge and dining area round out the space. The massive central bar, faced with stained oak and highlighted by chrome buttons, helps establish the functional zones. The solid maple butcher-block top floats upon the structure, and is echoed on tabletops; a tufted ceiling minimizes the din. Frank Lloyd Wright-inspired flagstone columns, wood panels and curving walls finished in silver foil complete the aura of modernity.

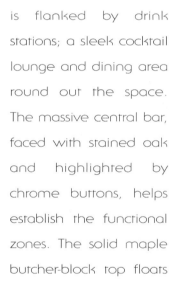

interior designer: II BY IV Design Associates Inc.
square feet/meters: 4,500/418 • design budget: not disclosed • seats: 150
photographer: David Whittaker

The sleek lounge is anchored by a curved banquette, backed by a silver foil finish that rises to the ceiling. Instead of scaling down the massive 4,500-square-foot space, designers chose to use the venue's expansive dimensions to create a sense of futuristic simplicity. Tables are well-spaced, furniture is spartan, and decorative elements are minimal. • The maple plank flooring is interrupted by a wave-like swirl of slate, and a series of mirrors and lights creates a pattern of repetition.

Uptown Brewery by Streets of New York
Tempe, Arizona

THE INTENT WAS TO TRANSFORM AN EXISTING EMPTY ESTABLISHMENT INTO A RESTAURANT WITH AN ECLECTIC 1930s NEW YORK CITY STREET THEME. THE ARCHITECT AND DESIGNERS COMPOSED THE URBAN AURA WITH COBBLESTONE STREETS, A BACK ALLEY, SIMULATED OUTDOOR PATIO, NEW YORK SKYLINE——EVEN A SUBWAY ENTRY. OTHER FEATURES INCLUDE A SEWER GATE WITH MEOWING CAT, AND LIVE TREES IN

a "Central Park" area. The focal point is a glass enclosed brewhouse in which copper and stainless steel equipment is highly visible from all areas of the dining room. The moderately priced menu and jovial atmosphere draw a mixed crowd: young couples with children and students from nearby Arizona State University. The bar layout incorporates a horseshoe-shaped, granite-topped bar, with the copper and brass tanks serving as part of the ambience. The entry to the bar features a wrought-iron canopy that represents a subway style entrance. The floor is a

warm wood set off by walls of brick and wood wainscoting. The rooms juxtapose old-world city elements such as street lamps, canopied murals and indoor trees, with heavily patterned industrial carpeting and sleek wooden booths. A skylight in the exposed ceiling allows light into the dining area. Most of the lighting, such as the street lamps, was selected to enhance the 1930s New York City motif. The overall effect is to transport patrons to another place, if only for the evening.

architect: **O'Dell & Associates** • interior designer: **Exclaim Design**
square feet/meters: 8,700/808 • design budget: not disclosed • seats: 275
photographer: **Mark Delsasso**

Leather booths and dining areas afford a prime view into the working brewhouse. The copper and stainless equipment is polished to a high shine. • A simulated outdoor bistro setting is complete with wrought-iron railings, canopied windows, street murals, and live trees. • Real cobble-stone paving, brick walls, window boxes, and shuttered windows create the feeling of walking down a street in another era.

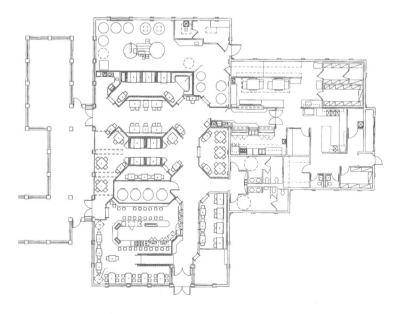

Tupelo Honey
Sea Cliff, New York

WHEN PATRONS STEP THROUGH THE DOORS AT TUPELO HONEY, THEY ARE ENGULFED BY A WAVE OF COLOR AND A ROOM THAT BUZZES WITH ENERGY. THE VENUE'S NAME IS INTENDED TO INVOKE IMAGES OF HOT CLIMATES ("TUPELO" IS A CITY IN MISSISSIPPI), FOOD ("HONEY"), AND MUSIC ("TUPELO HONEY" IS THE NAME OF A SONG BY VAN MORRISON). THE DESIGNER'S INTENTION WAS TO CREATE A

place where customers could feel like they are enjoying a night out on a tropical island. With the help of artists who designed and installed intricate glass mosaics on every surface imaginable, the architect wove a tropical tapestry throughout. Suspended in the center of the action is a massive stained-glass light fixture in the shape of a honeybee. Continuing the bee theme, the open kitchen features a fantastical wood-burning pizza oven that is designed in the form of a "beehive sand castle." Wrapping around the kitchen is a solid maple food bar, where one can observe food preparation or the bustle

of the dining area. Artists covered the 300 square feet of "wave" that undulates over the bars with approximately 40,000 individual pieces of colored stained glass, creating a mural of waves and sea creatures. On the back wall of the main bar is a large gold tinted oval mirror that was crafted to represent a setting sun, with mosaic accents which extend from each side of the mirror. In addition to the whimsical mosaic patterns, the restaurant is punctuated by casual furniture. Overhead, the ceiling is composed of noise-reducing acoustical foam in alternating squares assembled in the pattern of a honeycomb.

architect: **Diller + Patey Architects, PC** • interior designer: **David Pearson Design**
square feet/meters: **2,000/186** • design budget: **$200,000** • seats: **80**
photographer: **George Rugen**

Hand-cut mosaic tiles by artists Irene Inouye and Ron Shaffer, and blasts of color help to set the stage for a nightspot that buzzes with energy. The artists were having so much fun, they got swept away with the mosaic motif. Each table features a resplendent master-piece. ● Designers varied the floor materials to visually separate the bar and dining areas. The transition from tile to wood is further distinguished with curved geometric tile edging that echoes the undulating wave around the perimeter of the bar.

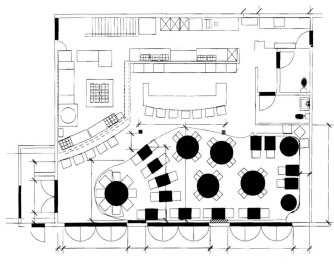

Directory

PUBS AND CLUBS

Bar Tiepolo
Hotel Europa & Regina
San Marco, 2159
Venice 30124 Italy
Tel: (39) 041-520-0477
Fax: (39) 041-523-1533

Big Shots
4511 McKinney Avenue
Dallas, Texas 75205
Tel: (214) 522-4808
Fax: (214) 522-4812

Bitter End B Side
311 Colorado Street
Austin, Texas 78701
Tel: (512) 478-2337
Fax: (512) 478-2462

Bunker
Via Domiziana Km 54/E 600
Pozzuoli, Naples 80078 Italy
Tel/Fax: (39) 081-866-5446

Carrot's Cafe
Pizza Euclide 1
Rome 00197 Italy
Tel: (39) 6-807-3876

Chart House
Hotel Inter-Continental Tokyo Bay
16-2 Kaigan 1-chome
Minato-Ku, Tokyo 105 Japan
Tel: (81) 3-5404-2222
Fax: (81) 3-5404-2111

Cheeky Monkey Cafe
14 Perry Mill Wharf
Newport, Rhode Island 02906
Tel: (401) 845-9494
Fax: (401) 841-9348

Churchill Bar
Churchill Inter-Continental London
30 Portman Square
London W1A 4ZX England
Tel: (44) 171-486-5800
Fax: (44) 171-486-1255

Fusion
240 Richmond Street West
Toronto, Ontario M5V 1V6 Canada
Tel: (416) 977-4116
Fax: (416) 977-4312

9
223 West 19th Street
New York, New York 10011
Tel: (212) 929-1085

The Garden of Eden
7080 Hollywood Boulevard
Hollywood, California 90028
Tel: (213) 465-3336
Fax: (213) 466-3336

The Gate
643 North La Cienega Boulevard
Los Angeles, California 90069
Tel: (310) 289-8808
Fax: (310) 289-5230

Hamiltons
New York New York Hotel
3790 Las Vegas Boulevard South
Las Vegas, Nevada 89109
Tel: (702) 740-6400
Fax: (702) 740-6444

Hollywood Athletic Club
6525 Sunset Boulevard
Hollywood, California 90028
Tel: (213) 962-6600
Fax: (213) 468-9109

Living Room
Rua Manuel Guedes, 474
São Paulo, São Paulo 01411-002 Brazil
Tel: (55) 11-866-6494
Fax: (55) 11-866-6445

Luxor Palace
City Hall Plaza
Cafe Prag Altmarkt 16-17
Dresden 8010 Germany
Tel: (49) 351-1057-6401
Fax: (49) 351-929-1645

MacArthur's
2171 Peachtree Street
Atlanta, Georgia 30309
Tel: (404) 352-3400
Fax: (404) 352-4770

Magazzini Generali
Via Pietrasanta, 14
Milan 20141 Italy
Tel: (39) 02-5521-1313
Fax: (39) 02-5521-3492

Met Bar
The Metropolitan Hotel
19 Old Park Lane
London W1Y 4LB England
Tel: (44) 171-447-5757
Fax: (44) 171-447-1100

Michael Jordan's™ The Restaurant
500 North LaSalle
Chicago, Illinois 60610
Tel: (312) 644-3865
Fax: (312) 644-3881

Michael's Club
Celebrity Cruises Galaxy Liner
5200 Blue Lagoon Drive
Miami, Florida 33126
Tel: (305) 262-6677
Fax: (305) 260-2040

Monsoon Café
1212 Third Street
Santa Monica, California 90403
Tel: (310) 576-9996
Fax: (310) 576-9988

Payard Patisserie and Bistro
1032 Lexington Avenue
New York, New York 10021
Tel: (212) 717-5252
Fax: (212) 717-0986

Props
911 East Morehead Street
Charlotte, North Carolina 28204
Tel: (704) 333-2226
Fax: (704) 333-2206

Rave
125 West 43rd Street
New York, New York 10036

Southend Brewery & Smokehouse
2100 South Boulevard
Charlotte, North Carolina 28203
Tel: (704) 358-4677
Fax: (704) 358-9960

Speakeasy
412 Congress Avenue
Austin, Texas 78701
Tel: (512) 476-8017
Fax: (512) 476-3143

Stage Left
Riverport Casino Center
Maryland Heights, Missouri 63043
Tel: (314) 770-8238
Fax: (314) 770-8399

The Summit
NationsBank Building
15 West Sixth Street
Tulsa, Oklahoma 74119
Tel: (918) 582-5243
Fax: (918) 585-1859

Superior
253 Yonge Street
Toronto, Ontario M5B 1N8 Canada
Tel: (416) 214-0416
Fax: (416) 214-9785

Tableaux Lounge
Sunroser Dia Kanyama
Tokyo 150 Japan
Tel: (81) 3-5489-2202
Fax: (81) 3-5489-2506

Tupelo Honey
39 Roslyn Avenue
Sea Cliff, New York 11579
Tel: (516) 671-8300
Fax: (516) 671-3902

Uptown Brewery by Streets of New York
1470 East Southern Avenue
Tempe, Arizona 85281
Tel: (602) 777-9600
Fax: (602) 955-8772

V2
131-133 Holland Park Avenue
London W11 3FH England
Tel: (44) 171-471-3000
Fax: (44) 171-603-4796

The Wave
University of Western Ontario
London, Ontario N6A 3K7 Canada
Tel: (519) 661-3007
Fax: (519) 661-3931

ZaZa
2063 Yonge Street
Toronto, Ontario M4S 2A2 Canada
Tel: (416) 488-2319
Fax: (416) 488-6950

Zoom Caffe and Bar
18 King Street East
Toronto, Ontario M5C 1C4 Canada
Tel: (416) 861-9872
Fax: (416) 861-9251

ZuZu's Coffee Bar
103 Pratt Street
Hartford, Connecticut 06103
Tel: (860) 244-8233
Fax: (860) 244-8235

ARCHITECTS & INTERIOR DESIGNERS

Stan Brent
10850 Riverside Drive
North Hollywood, California 91602
Tel: (818) 762-8697
Fax: (818) 762-9448

Giancarlo Brusati
Dorsoduro 2537
Venice 30123 Italy
Tel: (39) 041-520-3221
Fax: (39) 041-522-8641

Burbidge design/construction
  Richard Burbidge
156 West Brookline Street
Boston, Massachusetts 02118
Tel: (617) 536-9191
Fax: (617) 266-8775

Ciccotti Arredamenti Negozi s.r.l.
  Francesco Ciccotti
Via Giovanni Armenise
Rome 00131 Italy
Tel: (39) 06-413-0055
Fax: (39) 06-419-3976

Creative Consultants
  Tiffany Craven
1411 West Sixth Street
Austin, Texas 78703
Tel: (512) 478-7975
Fax: (512) 478-8282

Cricket Design Company Inc.
235 Carlaw Avenue
Toronto, Ontario M4M 2S1 Canada
Tel: (416) 463-1874
Fax: (416) 466-2244

David L. Downey Inc.
2901 South Highland
Las Vegas, Nevada 89109
Tel: (702) 873-8505
Fax: (702) 794-3529

David Pearson Design
  David Pearson
1600 Oregon Street
Orlando, Florida 32803
Tel: (407) 895-0444
Fax: (407) 898-8489

Desiderata
  Don Stewart
8024 West Third Street
Los Angeles, California 90048
Tel: (310) 852-4891
Fax: (310) 852-4811

Dick Clark Architecture
  Dick Clark • Jay Corder
  Kevin Gallagher
207 West Fourth Street
Austin, Texas 78701
Tel: (512) 472-4980
Fax: (512) 472-4991

Diller + Patey Architects, PC
708 Glen Cove Avenue
Glen Head, New York 11545
Tel: (516) 674-8200
Fax: (516) 674-9648

Engstrom Design Group
  Katy Hallal, AIA • Jennifer Johanson, AIA
  Susan Snow
1414 Fourth Street
San Rafael, California 94901
Tel: (415) 454-2277
Fax: (415) 454-2278

Ergo Design Works Inc.
  Lory Johansson • June Robinson Scott, ASID
8112½ West Third Street "D"
Los Angeles, California 90048
Tel: (213) 658-8901
Fax: (213) 658-8903

Exclaim Design
  Kim Dudley • Nichol Saulino
2817 East Camelback Road
Phoenix, Arizona 85016
Tel: (602) 955-4228
Fax: (602) 955-8772

George Hamilton Production
  Kevin Corn
139 South Beverly
Beverly Hills, California 90212
Tel: (310) 278-6578
Fax: (310) 278-3134

Massimo Josa Ghini
Via Caprarie 7
Bologna 40124 Italy
Tel: (39) 051-236563
Fax: (39) 051-237712

Gian Carlo Soresina, S-L-1, s.r.l.
Via Pietrasanta 14
Milan 20141 Italy
Tel: (39) 02-5521-1313
Fax: (39) 02-5521-3492

Global Dining
  Takeshi Miyamoto
7-1-5 Minami Aoyama
Minato-Ku, Tokyo 107 Japan
Tel: (81) 3-3407-0561
Fax: (81) 3-3407-0779

Gnosis Architettura
Francesco Buonfantino • Antonio Di Martino
Rossano Pandolfo
Via Toledo, 368
Naples 80132 Italy
Tel: (39) 081-552-3312
Fax: (39) 081-552-2558

Hirsch-Bedner Associates
Michael Bedner • Anna-Christine Brattel
Etienne Decluda • Diana Kawaguchi
Alex Kravner • Bill Nicol • Tamara Sypuli
3216 Nebraska Avenue
Santa Monica, California 90404
Tel: (310) 829-9087
Fax: (310) 453-1182

Hirsch-Bedner Associates
Chuck Chewning • Angela Denney
Howard Pharr
909 West Peachtree Street
Atlanta, Georgia 30309
Tel: (404) 873-4379
Fax: (404) 872-3588

Hirschberg Design Group Ltd.
Martin Hirschberg • Robert Lozowy
334 Queen Street East
Toronto, Ontario M5A 1S8 Canada
Tel: (416) 868-1210
Fax: (416) 868-6650

Hixson Design
Gary Hixson • Ginger Riley • Julie Wright
1414 East Fifth Street
Charlotte, North Carolina 28204
Tel: (704) 334-8088

James L. Bartholomew, Architect
James L. Bartholomew
220 West 19th Street
New York, New York 10011
Tel: (212) 645-0126
Fax: (212) 645-0290

Jean-Pierre Heim & Associates Inc.
Jean-Pierre Heim
24 rue Vieille du Temple
Paris 75004 France
Tel: (33) 1-4887-0708
Fax: (33) 1-4277-0181

Jean-Pierre Heim & Associates Inc.
Jean-Pierre Heim
160 Central Park South
New York, NY 10019
Tel: (212) 315-4346
Fax: (212) 582-1386

Maggie Gordon Design, Inc.
Maggie Gordon
20 Upton Avenue
Providence, Rhode Island 02906
Tel: (401) 751-1787
Fax: (401) 841-9348

Malholtra Nicholson Architects
John Nicholson
256 Pallmall
London, Ontario N6A 5P6 Canada
Tel: (519) 673-1190
Fax: (519) 673-1490

Mark Pinney Associates
Mark Pinney
125 Kensington High Street
London W8 5SF England
Tel: (44) 171-937-9789
Fax: (44) 171-937-3933

Davide Mercatali
Via Molino Delle Armi 45
Milan 12 Italy
Tel: (39) 02-836-0220
Fax: (39) 02-8940-5173

Nihon Sekkei, Inc.
International Division
2-1-1 Shinjuku Mitsui Building
Shinjuku-ku, Tokyo 160 Japan

O'Brien + Associates Design Inc.
Margaret O'Brien • Loren Atreide
Sam Cardella • Paul Collett
Beth Schnierow
222 Washington Avenue
Santa Monica, California 90403
Tel: (310) 458-9177
Fax: (310) 451-0812

O'Dell & Associates
Ken O'Dell
4203 East Indian School Road
Phoenix, Arizona 85018
Tel: (602) 954-7945
Fax: (602) 954-7947

Paul Draper and Associates, Inc.
Paul Draper
4106 Swiss Avenue
Dallas, Texas 75204
Tel: (214) 824-8352
Fax: (214) 824-0932

Rockwell Group
5 Union Square West
New York, New York 10003
Tel: (212) 463-0334
Fax: (212) 463-0335

Rosenberg Kolb Architects, PC
Eric Rosenberg • Michele Kolb
164 East 91st Street
New York, New York 10128
Tel: (212) 996-3099
Fax: (212) 996-3097

Seiber Design, Inc.
Ed Seiber • Mark Davis • Laurie Lee
Tim Nichols • Stan Shipley
675 Drewry Street
Atlanta, Georgia 30306
Tel: (404) 875-6765
Fax: (404) 875-0324

Shelton, Mindel & Associates
Lee F. Mindel, AIA • Peter L. Shelton
216 West 18th Street
New York, New York 10011
Tel: (212) 243-3939
Fax: (212) 727-7310

Shook Design Group, Inc.
Michael Dunning • Tom Goodwin
Kevin E. Kelley • George Price
Frank Quattrochi • Cicely Worrell
2000 South Boulevard
Charlotte, North Carolina 28210
Tel: (704) 377-0661
Fax: (704) 377-0953

Studio Arthur de Mattos Casas
Arthur de Mattos Casas
Alameda Ministro
Rocha Azevedo, 1052
São Paulo, São Paulo 01410-002 Brazil
Tel: (55) 11-282-6311
Fax: (55) 11-282-6608

Synar Design Group
Larry Synar, ASID
4110 East 21st Place
Tulsa, Oklahoma 74114-2111
Tel: (918) 749-3401
Fax: (918) 587-8601

Taylor Scott Architects
Kenneth R. Alexander, AIA
1437 South Boulder Avenue
Tulsa, Oklahoma 74119
Tel: (918) 587-8600
Fax: (918) 587-8601

II BY IV Design Associates Inc.
77 Mowat Avenue
Toronto, Ontario M6K 3E3 Canada
Tel: (416) 531-2224
Fax: (416) 531-4460

United Designers
Keith Hobbs • Linzi Coppick
37 Shad Thames
London SE1 2NJ England
Tel: (44) 171-357-6006
Fax: (44) 171-357-8008

Zakaspace
Spiros Zakas • Mark Geftman
Karen Hanlan
533 Northeast 13th Street
Fort Lauderdale, Florida 33304
Tel: (954) 728-8444
Fax: (954) 728-8443

PHOTOGRAPHERS

Jaime Ardiles-Arce
730 Fifth Avenue
New York, New York 10019
Tel: (212) 333-8779
Fax: (212) 593-2070

Bardagjy Photography
Paul Bardagjy
4111 B Marathon
Austin, Texas 78756
Tel: (512) 452-9636
Fax: (512) 452-6425

Beck Peccoz/Fasano
Marco Beck Peccoz
Via Costodi 16
Milan 20141 Italy
Tel: (39) 02-5521-1313
Fax: (39) 02-5521-3492

Alex Brattel
23A Limehouse Court
Morris Road, London E14 GNT
England
Tel: (44) 171 987 0590

David Brittain
c/o United Designers
37 Shad Thames
London SE1 2NJ England
Tel: (44) 1284-830316

Dan Cornish Photography
Dan Cornish
44 Old Ridgefield Road
Wilton, Connecticut 06897
Tel: (203) 762-9517
Fax: (203) 762-9518

David Whittaker Photography
David Whittaker
444 Heath Street East
Toronto, Ontario M4G 1B5 Canada
Tel: (416) 429-0245
Fax: (416) 429-0135

Paul Dennler
1137 Sixth Street
Santa Monica, California 90403
Tel: (310) 319-1538
Fax: (310) 451-0812

Dot Griffith Photography
Dot Griffith
1117 North Virginia Avenue
Atlanta, Georgia 30306
Tel/Fax: (404) 872-8524

Tim Evans-Cook
c/o United Designers
37 Shad Thames
London SE1 2NJ England
Tel: (44) 171-357-6006
Fax: (44) 171-357-8008

The Factory
Richard Bryant
2 Acre Road
Kingston on Thames
Surrey KT2 6EF England
Tel: (44) 181-546-4352
Fax: (44) 181-541-5230

Francesca Francisci
Via Mario Rapisardi 42
Rome 00137 Italy
Tel: (39) 06-827-8215

David Glomb
458½ North Genesee Avenue
Los Angeles, California 90036
Tel: (323) 655-4491
Fax: (323) 651-1437

Interior Images
Richard Johnson
2 Glengannon Drive
Toronto, Ontario M4B 2W4 Canada
Tel: (416) 755-7742
Fax: (416) 755-9622

Dennis Krukowski
329 East 92nd Street
New York, New York 10128
Tel: (212) 860-0912
Fax: (212) 860-0913

Nacása & Partners Inc.
Atsushi Nakamichi
3-5-5 Minami Azabu
Minato-Ku, Tokyo 106-0047 Japan
Tel: (81) 3-3444-2922
Fax: (81) 3-3444-2678

Paul Warchol Photography
Paul Warchol
224 Centre Street
New York, New York 10013
Tel: (212) 431-3461
Fax: (212) 274-1953

Richard Klein Photography
Richard Klein
2220 South Harwood
Dallas, Texas 75215
Tel: (214) 421-1555
Fax: (214) 428-7145

Rotili & De Simone
Francesco Rotili • Piero De Simone
Via Augusto Righi Strada
Privata Patroni Griffi, 42
Naples 80125 Italy
Tel: (39) 081-570-3026
Fax: (39) 081-570-3024

Rugen Pictures
George Rugen
15 West 28th Street
New York, New York 10001
Tel: (212) 979-8200
Fax: (212) 979-8270

Jan Staller
161 Charles Street
New York, New York 10014
Tel: (212) 633-8370
Fax: (212) 633-0848

Steinkamp/Ballogg
Mark Ballogg
664-6 West Hubbard Street
Chicago, Illinois 60610
Tel: (312) 421-1233
Fax: (312) 421-1241

Reyndell Stockman
43 Maple Street
Orleans, Vermont 05860
Tel: (802) 754-2718

Studio Arcadia
Fabrice Rambert
55 rue Kilford
Courbevoie 92400 France
Tel: (33) 1-4334-2828
Fax: (33) 1-4333-9100

Tim Buchman Photography
Tim Buchman
1311-L Corton Drive
Charlotte, North Carolina 28203
Tel/Fax: (704) 376-8580

Tuca Reinés Estudio Fotográfico
Tuca Reinés
Rua Emanuel Kant, 58
São Paulo, São Paulo
Brazil 05436-050
Tel: (55) 11-3061-9127
Fax: (55) 11-852-8735

Visus Ltd.
Mark Delsasso
5120 North 83rd Street
Scottsdale, Arizona 85250
Tel: (602) 946-4443
Fax: (602) 946-4445

Young Company
Hank Young
923 West 24th Street
Kansas City, Missouri 64108
Tel: (816) 221-7376
Fax: (816) 842-4068

YUM
Ron Manville
35 Peeptoad Road
North Scituate, Rhode Island 02857
Tel/Fax: (401) 934-1996

Wade Zimmerman
9 East 97th Street
New York, New York 10029
Tel: (212) 427-8784
Fax: (212) 427-3526

Index